QA5-749

SOCIAL DEVELOPMENT
IN CHILDHOOD

Previous volumes based on the annual Hyman Blumberg Symposia on Research in Early Childhood Education (available in both paperbound and clothbound editions)

Julian C. Stanley, general series editor

SOCIAL DEVELOPMENT IN CHILDHOOD:
Day-Care Programs and Research

Edited by Roger A. Webb

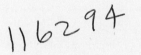

THE JOHNS HOPKINS UNIVERSITY PRESS
BALTIMORE AND LONDON

Manufactured in the United States of America

The Johns Hopkins University Press, Baltimore, Maryland 21218
The Johns Hopkins Press Ltd., London

Library of Congress Catalog Number 77-4778
ISBN 0-8018-1946-6 hardcover
ISBN 0-8018-1947-4 paperback

Library of Congress Cataloging in Publication data
will be found on the last printed page of this book.

*To Alvin Nye Main, whose untimely death left all of us who
knew him with a sense of great personal loss*

CONTRIBUTORS

Mary C. Blehar, Department of Psychology, University of Virginia, Charlottesville

Phyllis T. Elardo, Department of Educational Foundations, University of Arkansas at Little Rock

Esther Blank Greif, Department of Psychology, Boston University

Frances S. Harnick, Department of Psychology, University of New Mexico, Albuquerque

Mary B. Main, Department of Psychology, University of California, Berkeley

Pamela J. Mills, School of Education, University of Massachusetts, Amherst

Mary Ellen Oliveri, Center for Family Research, George Washington University Medical Center

Craig T. Ramey, Frank Porter Grahm Child Development Center, University of North Carolina, Chapel Hill

Roger A. Webb, Department of Psychology, University of Arkansas at Little Rock

Contents

PREFACE

This volume contains the papers from the Fourth Hyman Blumberg Symposium on Research in Early Childhood Education. The symposium series is supported by the income from a generous gift from the Amalgamated Clothing Workers of America to the Johns Hopkins University. The gift and the symposium it supports are both a tribute to the late Hyman Blumberg, a former executive vice-president of the ACWA, and a symbol of the Union's lasting commitment to high-quality child care. The symposium series has been in progress since 1971 under the general direction of Professor Julian Stanley, who also edited the first volumes in the series. All of us involved with the project acknowledge Professor Stanley's generous assistance and guidance.

The earlier volumes in the Blumberg series have dealt with a variety of matters, but generally with the intellectual development of young children. The first two volumes in the series remain the major source for a number of intervention studies that have not been so thoroughly described in any other publication. The present volume changes direction slightly from the previous thrust of the series and turns to the problems of the social development of children—with a particular interest in those who are involved in various group-care situations. While there is hardly a consensus among students of educational intervention on the benefits of programs directed at intellectual growth, the associated problems of social development have only recently been considered at all. It is my contention that the social aspects of group-care for young children hold both more potential threat and greater promise for the future of children in our society than do the intellectual aspects.

The papers that make up the volume represent a variety of points of view all related to the problems of intervention into social development. Some of the papers are basic theoretical contributions, while others are overtly applied in orientation. In my introduction, I will try to show what I see to be the relevance of these varied contributions to the problem at hand.

ACKNOWLEDGMENTS

In addition to the financial support provided by Hyman Blumberg Symposium fund and the help of Professor Julian Stanley mentioned in the Preface, the authors wish to gratefully acknowledge the following sources of support and assistance.

Mary Blehar wishes to express her appreciation to Professor Mary Ainsworth and Professor Julian Stanley for their invaluable suggestions and critical comments.

Mary Main's work was supported in part by a grant from the National Science Foundation and in part by a Biomedical Sciences Support Grant. Dr. Main expresses her thanks to Alan Sroufe and Phyllis Levin for their helpful comments.

The work of Webb, Oliveri, and Harnick was supported by a grant from the Robert Sterling Clark Foundation of New York and a contract with the Baltimore City Public Schools. Mary Ellen Oliveri's study was supported by the Edith Castleberry Endowed Fellowship of the American Association of University Women Educational Foundation. Carol Leininger helped with much of the data collection and analysis.

The work of Craig Ramey and Pamela Mills was supported by grant number HD–03110 from the National Institute of Child Health and Human Development.

Esther Blank Greif wishes to thank Shelley Cohen Konrad and Freda Rebelsky for their helpful comments on her manuscript.

Phyllis Elardo's work was supported by Grant number SF–500, Children's Bureau, Department of Health, Education, and Welfare and by a grant from the Rockefeller Brothers Fund. Dr. Elardo expresses her appreciation to Professor Bettye Caldwell both for seeing the need for AWARE and for support in developing the program.

Sandie Bond typed much of the manuscript of this book. Her careful work and good nature were much appreciated.

INTRODUCTION

The ways in which we raise our children represent cultural patterns that have evolved over centuries to meet basic human needs. One fact of human life is that our species has an extended period of immaturity during which the young must be cared for by others and must learn those things required to be fully competent members of the species and of the particular community to which they belong. Providing care and instruction for its young is a requirement for any human society, and a society that fails in this task will not survive. Care and instruction must be delivered, however, in a fashion consistent with the limits imposed on the culture by its environment, technology, and ecology. Thus, child rearing is a compromise between the needs of children and the other demands on parental time and energy.

When I say that child-rearing techniques have evolved, there is an implication that the ways in which we rear our children are not particularly logical, nor even well understood, but that they have met a functional test over an extended time. When we change the ways in which we raise our children, we necessarily venture into an area with few guidelines. It is proper in such a case to ask whether we might be doing harm—possibly exceeding the capacity of the species to adapt. That is not to say that change is necessarily bad. Humankind—along with the rat and cockroach—is one of God's more adaptable creatures and has thrived under a great variety of conditions. Moreoever, there is no evidence that what we do now is in any way optimal. The point, rather, is that how we raise our children is a serious matter, and we lack sufficient knowledge to change our current practices with any confidence. What we require is a more thorough knowledge of how social development actually takes place.

For those of us concerned with the psychological implications of child care and vice versa, our basic scientific literature has—at least up until recently—seemed oddly out of touch with the actual situation we face. Our research has been designed around a particular "hypothetical" child. This child lives at home with his mother until he is three or four years old and then only enters group-care on a part-time basis. His parents treat him warmly and permissively to encourage his sense of responsibility and control. The child's father works at a responsible and rewarding job to support the family, but is regularly available as an authority figure and model of the male role. The child's personality is viewed largely as a matter of parental input, and the role of peers or societal institutions is minimal until the school years. If the child attends nursery school prior to kindergarten, it is largely to assist him in breaking down the bonds of dependency and egocentrism that would prevent him from functioning in a group situation. The educational requirements of nursery school are minimal, since by the time our child enters school he will be already reasonably well educated and socialized.

The facts of our society are, of course, no longer in line with this model of the child. Our government tells us that perhaps 20 percent of the families in our society fall below a line that defines poverty and that these families produce an inordinate proportion of our young. About a quarter of first marriages end in divorce. A recent television program on the "children of divorce" estimated that if current trends continue, in the not so distant future, the majority of children in our society will be the products of broken homes. The proportion of the work force that is female is approaching 50 percent, of which a substantial number are single heads of households. Even within intact homes in which the wife does not have a full-time job, fewer children are being reared entirely at home. Another investigator and I are presently trying to find a group of home-reared children for a study we want to do. "Home-reared" is probably going to be defined as not more than six hours a week in group care because, as far as we can tell, children who are at home with their mothers more than that no longer exist in substantial numbers. Schools complain that increasing numbers of children reach them totally unprepared for educational experiences. In short, the hypothetical child around whom our psychology is based is becoming increasingly the exception rather than the rule.

Closely associated with our assumption of a "norm"—as defined by our hypothetical child—is the assumption that those not conforming to the norm are "abnormal." Now this, of course, is true in a statistical sense, but our brothers in the mental health areas have done a better job than we of differentiating the statistical concept from its pejorative implications. In other words, we still tend to see the norm as the ideal and measure success and failure, illness and health, by how far one falls from the norm. This criticism clearly applies to some of the papers in this volume—including my own—but it is probably time to look carefully at the extent to which our interpretations of our findings simply reflect our equation of "normal" with "good."

If we are to escape the domination of the normal in our thinking, we require a clearer notion of the processes that lead to the behavior patterns we see in our society. The description of individual differences has long been psychology's stock in trade, primarily because we have had little better to do. The papers that have been selected for this volume represent, in my opinion, three significant, recent, changes in our understanding of how social development takes place. These may be described briefly as the application of attachment theory to the problems of early child care, the application of role theory to social development, and the realization that the distinction between intellectual and social-emotional that most of us make so easily is an essentially false dichotomy.

Since the publication of the seminal "Nature of the child's tie to his mother," Bowlby and others—particularly Mary Ainsworth in this country—have demonstrated that in his social development the human infant goes through a sequence of interactions with his caretakers that appear to be biologically determined and that constitute critical experience for normal development. The stages thus described are closely analogous to similar stages seen in the development of other species, with the other large primates being most highly similar. The analysis of attachment theory implies that the human infant has certain expectations about the nature of the care he is to receive and that these expectations may be violated only with attendant risk to the well-being of the child. The insights of attachment theory have been perhaps the most important recent contribution to our understanding of intrapsychic phenomena. Where Freud taught us that we confront authority as a little boy faces his father, Bowlby teaches that we face insecurity and loneliness as a little child who is lost from his mother. Not surprisingly perhaps, attachment theorists have been among the most conservative and pessimistic about the use of group-care for young children.

In the present volume the papers by Mary Blehar and Mary Main represent applications of the attachment perspective to the problems of early child care. Blehar's paper is an expansion of her earlier report of the effects of early day-care on the social development of two- and three-year-olds. Her study is distinctive and important because it seems to be the first clear claim of adverse consequences to the social attachments of young children resulting from day-care. There are problems in interpreting the study to be sure. Her study is not a true experiment—nor is any other study in this field at the moment—since the groups are self-selected, and, in spite of her efforts to demonstrate the equal maternal sensitivity of the groups, there is the suspicion that families who choose to put their children in day-care may be systematically different from those who do not. In fact, one might easily argue that the consistent finding by Ainsworth and her group of differences in maternal behaviors that relate to strange situation behavior must mean that differences in strange situation behavior similar to those reported by Blehar must of necessity indicate differences in maternal behavior. The argument follows directly from an assumption that the strange situation is a valid measure. Also, there is the possibility that since Blehar studied her sample a relatively short time after they first entered day-care, she might be studying the reaction to the beginning of day-care and not the long-term adjustment.

In spite of these qualifications, it is hard to escape the conclusion that Blehar's study is the best done of its type to date and must be taken seriously. There are two primary reasons for this. First, she has studied reasonably well-to-do, middle-class, children who are in day-care through the choice of their parents. The homes from which these children come are what those of us in the field generally call "advantaged." This is in striking contrast to other studies that have used poor children, for whom day-care is confounded with a number of other concerns. Second, the Blehar study is marked by a sophistication and subtlety of measurement that is characteristic of the Ainsworth group generally. Thus, when reading the study, one should not become overly concerned with the separation protest data—the measure that most studies in the area focus on—but should concentrate on the ambivalence shown during the reunion episodes of the strange situation. It is in these behaviors that Blehar finds the most consistent difference between her day-care and home-reared groups.

Mary Main underlines the seriousness of Blehar's findings and expands on their possible interpretation in a major theoretical paper on the child's avoidance of its mother. I do not want to detract from Main's eloquent and orderly presentation of her thesis with a paraphrase, but her central theme of "avoidance indicates conflict" suggests that the child's avoidance of its mother under stress may be a more serious indication of difficulties than either protest or indifference. The correlations of avoidance with other behavioral measures that Main presents are among the highest and most consistent in the literature. Also, Main's interweaving of human experimental and clinical studies with work from the ethological tradition constitutes, in my opinion, a masterful example of the power of a truly comparative approach to a psychological problem.

In spite of my admiration and respect for the line of research represented in the papers by Blehar and Main, I do have some difficulties with the central metaphors of the attachment perspective. Like their psychoanalytic forebears, attachment theorists are applying the language of pathology to what many of us would consider normal behavior. It is not altogether surprising that the resulting descriptions have a pathological tone to them. Thus, in Blehar's paper the model to which day-care experiences are compared is the Bowlby–Robertson detachment model that describes the stages a child goes through when an established attachment bond is broken. The suggestion of the Blehar approach is that perhaps, day-care represents a series of separation experiences that have the total effect of a longer, more serious, break in the attachment bond. The ambivalence—anger and avoidance—shown by the child in the strange situation is analogous to the rejection and anger shown by the child to the attachment object after an extended absence. Is this a proper and adequate analogy for describing the day-care experience? My own intuition tells me that it is not. Moreover, the failure to find evidence of increases in gross pathology in day-care groups or even any differences in social development in studies like that of Caldwell and her associates argues that day-care per se is not the problem.

Blehar herself argues that differences in the quality of day-care are clearly possible and that it must not be considered a uniform experience. More importantly, I think, day-care must not be considered an independent variable in the experimental sense of the term. The decision to place a child in day-care is one additional variable that constitutes part of a family situation. The reasons that lead a mother to put her children into day-care or to stay home with them are probably more important than the simple day-care versus no day-care dichotomy.*

The paper by Ramey and Mills—and to a lesser degree the paper by Oliveri, Harnick, and myself—deals with group-care under drastically different conditions from those studied by Blehar. In the Ramey and Mills study, what is essentially a day-care center is used as a social and educational institution to modify the circumstances of childrens' lives. While we cannot know directly the reasons that mothers overwhelmingly accepted the offer to participate in the program, we may surmise that it was at least in part to obtain the numerous financial and medical benefits included as parts of the program. We might think of these families as paid participants in a study rather than individuals who have voluntarily decided to put their children into day-care. Also, of course, the homes that these children are coming from are much less ideal than those represented in the Blehar study.

While we do not know to which of many differences between the Blehar study and the Ramey and Mills study to attribute the

---

*Since the preparation of the Main and Blehar chapters, a paper by Brookhart and Hock (*Child Development*, 1976, 47, 333–40) has appeared and should be noted. Using Ainsworth's scales and a replication of the strange situation, Brookhart and Hock found no differences in rated avoidance between home-reared and day-care 10- to 12-month-old infants, but did find more avoidance when the infants in both rearing conditions were tested at home rather than in a laboratory setting. These authors offer the interesting alternative that avoidance might be better considered a sign of independence than of conflict. While the exact relevance of this new study to the problem at hand is not clear, three points should be noted. The sample studied by Brookhart and Hock was younger than the samples used by the Ainsworth group, there is a likely sensitization effect due to repeated measures, and the absolute level of avoidance seen by Brookhart and Hock was a good deal lower—by a factor of two or three—than the comparable data obtained by the Ainsworth group.

outcomes—and while we have no directly comparable data—it would appear that the reactions of the two groups to group-care are quite different. Ramey and Mills found that not only did their program produce apparent gains in intellectual growth, but it also improved the interaction between infants and their mothers. Moreover, the changes in mother-infant interaction that Ramey and Mills found are precisely those that might be expected to improve the quality of the relationship by increasing the mother's sensitivity to her child. In short, it would appear highly unlikely that Blehar's findings would replicate within Ramey and Mills' "high-risk" groups. Roughly, the same conclusion could be reached through an examination of the data reported by Oliveri, Harnick, and myself. Our two intervention programs that involved young children in group-care situations seemed to produce their major effects in the areas of language use, imitation, and social competence—again, those areas that would seem to imply some sensitivity in interaction between child and caretaker.

The relationship between intellectual invervention programs and social effects that is seen in the Ramey and Mills paper and in the work of Webb, Oliveri, and Harnick leads to the second major theme of the volume. In the work of Esther Blank Greif and Phyllis Elardo, we see examples of the application of role theory to the social development of children. In Greif's paper, the concern is with the earliest examples of role playing and role taking, while Elardo's work is fundamentally an application of the role-playing perspective to the problems of moral behavior in a school setting. In both papers the point of departure is the Piagetian concept of egocentrism, though the direction taken thereafter is vastly different.

The notion that social and moral development consists at least in part of the ability to take the point of view of another is widespread. Piaget seems to have borrowed the concept of the generalized other and its importance in the development of the self-concept from G. H. Mead. What is interesting is that Piaget places the critical event—the use of another to map out one's own body schema—at the transition between state III and IV of the sensory-motor period—around the age of ten months to a year. Thus, according to Piaget, the child's ability to see himself in terms of others emerges very early in his life. Unfortunately, the implications of some of Piaget's other early work seem to have had a greater effect on our conception of the child's social development. The concept of egocentrism, the child's inability to describe events from another's perspective or to take into account the knowledge that another possesses, and the prevalence of parallel play have led us to think of the young child as a relatively unsocial little character, and nothing could be further from the truth.

Using a technique borrowed from linguistics and reminiscent of the work of Mueller and Catherine Garvey, Greif has attempted to discover principles underlying the young child's social interaction by analyzing recurring patterns in his language. What is surprising about Greif's results is the prevalence of overt role-assigning and role-playing in these young children's interactions. One is left with the suspicion that these children somehow know that one of their important tasks is to understand and practice various adult roles and that they take the task very seriously. Woe be unto the child who takes a role and then fails to play it out consistently. One is also reminded in all of this of the regret and concern expressed by Bronfenbrenner over the failure of our society to provide our children with the opportunity to see adults in a multitude of roles.

The ability to take the role of another is something we must presumably learn through example and practice, and a lack of these experiences is as much a form of deprivation as the intellectual deficits to which we have given so much attention in recent years. Elardo's paper is a novel attempt to program such experiences for a group of elementary school children. Both the problems she experienced in implementing the program and the reactions of the children are instructive. The encouraging feature of Elardo's paper is the hope it holds for effecting some change in children's social and moral outlooks by incorporating such matters into the curriculum.

Before leaving these papers on role taking and role playing, one final point should be noted. There is a discrepancy in the language used in the papers by Elardo and Greif, and I have made no attempt to force a resolution. The use of "egocentric" and "sociocentric" by these two writers implies a conflict that is more apparent than real. Of course, Piaget's use of the term "egocentric" does not imply anything about whether one is social or not. The term refers to the tendency of us all to confuse our own intellectual constructions with objective reality. Whether we use the term to describe all our dealings with the world, or only our dealings with the social world, as Greif and Elardo are doing, it is clear that what "egocentric" means changes over time. As I mentioned above, Piaget places the first major breakthrough at ten months of age. Greif's data show that by the age of three children are reasonably competent at consciously taking the role of another. Children are not very good, however, at communicating their perceptions to another person, nor are they very good at taking into account what information another person might possess. This is only to say that egocentrism is not a unitary concept, but is something that develops as a matter of qualitative change over a number of years.

This point takes me back to the final major theme of the volume. All of the papers included here give evidence of the critical tie between a child's social development and his intellectual development. Whether we look at the matter from the impact of a child's social life on his intellectual development—as Ramey and Mills do—or from how a child's intellectual abilities constrain his social interactions—as Elardo does—we see how intimately related these topics are. As my associates and I have tried to show in our work, an appreciation of this relationship takes us much further into the processes by which both social and intellectual abilities develop, and it is the process that should concern us.

As things stand, most of us still fall short of dealing with process, and that is due in part to our preoccupations with normative considerations. Our attachment theorists, I have tried to show, are concerned with the norm of biological normalcy—a version, I think, of what Donald Campbell has recently called "romantic naturalism"—but the criticism applies equally well to Ramey and Mills and to my associates and me who take the intellectual norms of the white middle-class as the standard to which all children should conform. It is only as we break down our prejudices about norms as ideals that we will become able to examine the processes of development with a more open mind. Those of us involved in this project hope that this is one step in that direction.

SOCIAL DEVELOPMENT
IN CHILDHOOD

1

MOTHER-CHILD INTERACTION IN DAY-CARE AND HOME-REARED CHILDREN

Mary C. Blehar

In recent years, the demand for group day-care facilities has grown as more and more women with preschool children are seeking employment outside the home. The reasons for this return of women to the labor force derive both from economic pressures and from changes in attitudes. With the advent of the Women's Liberation Movement especially, many mothers have come to question the conventional wisdom that their proper place is in the home. Group day-care appeals to a wide range of parents who must find alternatives to individual home care for their children.

However convenient day-care may be as a solution to child-care problems, it has also generated considerable controversy. The idea of rearing young children in a group setting away from their mothers during the formative preschool years is still a relatively new concept in contemporary American society. Critics lament group day-care as a negative influence on children whom they see as isolated from family and neighborhood within the center's walls. Enthusiasts view it as an antidote to myriad social problems. Almost inevitably, day-care has become a hotly debated political issue, while questions about its effects on child development remain largely unanswered by research. Hopefully, however, empirical answers to these basic questions will ultimately determine whether group day-care is indeed a viable alternative to more conventional family rearing.

The purpose of this chapter is to examine group day-care as it may relate to one very significant influence in a young child's social development—namely, his attachment to his primary mother figure. Work undertaken by this author (Blehar 1974) on some differences in mother-child relations in day-care and home-reared children will also be reported. Because of the complex nature of this research area, these findings (and others discussed in this chapter) must necessarily be considered tentative and open to qualifications. But before discussing day care as it relates to attachment, it may be helpful to acquaint the reader with a theoretical framework for conceptualizing the development of mother-child relationships.

ATTACHMENT

Attachment is defined as an affectional bond that an infant forms with a mother figure (Ainsworth 1973). Under normal circumstances, he will become attached to that person with whom he has most social interaction (usually his natural mother), even if she is rejecting, provided there is sufficient interaction. Once the infant has formed an attachment—typically by seven months of age—he will maintain a degree of proximity to the attachment figure and will reliably protest separation from her, even if his basic physiological needs are gratified by other caregivers (Bowlby 1969).

The specific behaviors that mediate the attachment relationship change with age. Between seven months and two years of age (approximately), the child's relationship to the mother is based primarily upon physical proximity. That is, he seeks to keep himself within more or less close range of the mother and he protests separation. In the preschool years, overt manifestations of attachment behaviors cease to be displayed as often and at such high intensities. Cognitive representation of the mother and better understanding of her motivations now mediate the relationship (Bowlby 1969; Marvin 1971) so that a mother's explanation that she will be back soon is often enough to enable the child to cope easily with minor separations.

Bowlby (1969, 1973) has sought to explain attachment behaviors in terms of an ethological-evolutionary theory. According to

Earl

this theory, the infant's behavioral systems, especially those concerned with attachment, have genetic underpinnings, which cause behaviors to be stable across a wide variety of environments. The infant is genetically biased to become attached to a figure and genetically biased to protest separation. According to Bowlby, the behavioral systems which mediate infant-mother attachment evolved through a process of natural selection because they bestowed survival advantages on infants and young children in the environment in which the human species emerged. While the environment in most homes today contains relatively few of the selective pressures that led to that evolution, the genetic determinants of infant behavior have remained essentially unchanged. The child's behavior is labile, but there are limits to the environmental variations he can tolerate and still develop normally. If the environment deviates too widely from that to which he is evolutionarily adapted, then behavioral anomalies will result.

Attachment theory raises the question of how flexibly modern societies can arrange child care without working against the basic propensities for the formation and maintenance of attachment relationships. Reservations about group day-care stem from a concern that elements it involves, such as multiple mothering and/or mother-child separation,* may interfere with the development of normal attachments to the mother or disrupt already established relationships.

The idea of group day-care for infants has met with popular opposition because of findings that infants reared in 24-hour institutions where they were subjected to diffuse care-giving, could not form attachments, and later suffered deviant emotional development (Goldfarb 1943; Bender & Yarnell 1941; Provence & Lipton 1962). Can multiple mothering in group day care likewise weaken the primary attachment to the mother, or worse yet, leave the infant without an attachment to anyone?

One notable study has addressed itself to this issue. Caldwell and her associates (Caldwell, Wright, Honig, & Tannenbaum 1970) compared children who started group day-care at around one year

---

*Separation here and elsewhere refers to separation initiated by the child's attachment figure rather than by the child himself.

of age with children who had been reared at home by their mothers. On a number of variables purporting to measure strength of attachment, they found no differences between children in the two groups when they were thirty months of age. Caldwell qualified her results as pertaining only to day-care centers where staff-child ratios were low and where attention was paid to the individual infant's needs for intensive social interaction with stable figures. A more recent study by Kearsley, Zelazo, Kagan, and Hartmann (in press) found no difference in latency to cry upon separation from the mother between infants who had been enrolled in part-time day care from 3 1/2 months and a control group. These findings suggest that infants in group care can still form attachments of normal intensity to their mothers. However, full-time infant day-care is still regarded with caution because fears that erratic, impersonal, or unstimulating care could have profoundly adverse effects on children exposed to it during the critical first year of life.

The research conducted by this author (Blehar 1974) involved a study of qualitative aspects of attachment to the mother in older children, who had been at home with their mothers two or three years before starting group day-care. These children were already attached to their mothers by the time they were enrolled in day-care centers, so the possibility that multiple care-giving could weaken the attachment bond seemed quite remote. Group day-care was conceptualized as repeated daily mother-child separation and the possible influence of such separation on already established mother-child relationships was examined. Since the findings of this study are discussed with reference to a body of literature on the effects of separation on young children, a brief review of that literature will follow.

CHILDREN'S RESPONSES TO SEPARATIONS

In a classic study, Robertson and Bowlby (1952) observed three distinct phases in young children's reactions to major institutional separation. At the time of separation, most children in the sample were between ages one and four. Initially, there occurred a protest phase, followed by a despair phase, in which a child would reject attentions from substitute care-givers. If the separation continued for a long period of time and the child was not provided with an opportunity to form new attachments, he would manifest detachment. In this phase, he would regain interest in the environment, but when his mother would come to visit, he would show little or no interest in her as an attachment figure. Bowlby interpreted detachment as a defensive behavioral mechanism which stemmed from repression of anxiety and ambivalence toward the mother.

The child's response to reunion with the mother depended on the phase of response to separation he was in at the time. Children who were in the protest or despair phases responded to reunion with heightened attachment behaviors, intermingled with angry ambivalent behaviors. Eventually, however, they reestablished relationships of a more normal quality. Children who were in the detachment phase responsed to reunion with indifference. In some cases, they persisted in this mode indefinitely, and in others, detachment behaviors gave way to attachment behaviors of an anxious, ambivalent quality. Ainsworth (personal communication) had the opportunity to examine Robertson and Bowlby's data. She reported that the younger children in the sample (those between one and two and a half) were more likely to pass into detachment than the older children, who appeared more capable of maintaining an attachment to the mother, albeit of an anxious quality.

Adverse enduring effects of the type described above have been found chiefly in studies of long separation and in children under four or five years of age. However, reactions similar in form (although usually neither in intensity nor duration) have been reported in separations of days or weeks (Jessner, Blom, Waldfogel 1952; Prugh, Staub, Sands, Kirschbaum, & Lenihan 1963). Ainsworth and Bell (1970) have reported observing angry resistant behaviors and avoidance of the mother in one-year-old infants following very brief laboratory separation.

Besides the child's age and the duration of the separation, there are a number of other factors which can influence response to separation. Robertson and Robertson (1971) found that intensive warm foster care during separation can attenuate a child's distress. Yarrow (1961) found less distress if separations occurred in environments familiar to the child.

In summary, two types of response to major separation have been identified. The first is characterized by heightened attachment behaviors and sometimes by ambivalence, and the second is characterized by avoidant behaviors and apparent indifference to the mother. Elements of both reactions can be observed alternating in a given child, and detachment behaviors can give way to attachment behaviors. The significance of separation disturbances for social development varies in accordance with the intensity and duration of the disturbances. However, there appear to be certain prototypes of response that can be observed in separations of varying duration. Separation anxiety is caused by the absence of a specific figure rather than by unfulfilled physiological needs, but the intensity of protest and subsequent adverse effects are moderated by familiarity of environment and by response substitute care-givers.

THE EFFECTS OF DAILY SUBSTITUTE CARE

While a great deal is known about young children's reactions to institutional rearing and long separations, the effects of daily substitute care have been relatively unresearched. Reviews of the effects of maternal employment (e.g., Hoffman & Stolz 1961; Hoffman 1974) have tended to concentrate on maternal attitudes or have studied effects in a mixed age range of children, many of whose mothers had started working only after the children were in grade school. However, work by Moore (1964, 1969) dealt with the effects of various types of substitute care which had begun before age five on children's social behaviors at age seven or eight. Patterns of maternal employment were variable, ranging from part-time work begun in the child's fourth or fifth year to full-time work begun while the child was an infant. Moore was able to identify two samples of children, one in which substitute care had been stable and another in which care had been unstable. Children who had experienced unstable care had usually started it before their second birthdays. At age seven, they were conspicuously insecure and easily upset. They also received high ratings on measures of dependency and nervousness, and were reported as having more fears than other children. However, the parents were also described as unstable personalities, so there was a confounding of mode of care and parental behavior.

Children who had stable care before the second birthday tended to seek more attention from their mothers at age seven, and in some cases, mothers reported having failed to establish close relationships with them. Children who had stable care after age three showed no emotional difficulties. In Moore's study there was great variability in frequency of substitute care and also a confounding of parental personality with type of care, so that clear-cut interpretation of the results is difficult. However, the work is valuable in indicating that the effects of daily substitute care may depend on at least three variables: (1) the child's age at the time such care begins; (2) its stability; and (3) the type of enduring home environment the parents provide for the child.

THE STRANGE SITUATION:
A METHOD FOR ASSESSING QUALITY OF ATTACHMENT

In the present study, day-care separations were also considered as an event that could possibly distress young children and, in turn, affect the quality of attachment to the primary mother figure. In order to test this hypothesis, a technique sensitive to qualitative differences in mother-child interaction was needed. The strange situation (devised by Ainsworth and Wittig 1969) was chosen for this purpose. The strange situation first elicits exploratory behaviors and then, through a series of separations and reunions, heightens and intensifies attachment behaviors. The strange situation was originally developed in the course of a longitudinal study on the development of infant-mother attachment in the first year of life. Twenty-three infants who had been observed at home during the course of their first year were also observed in the situation at fifty-one weeks of age. Ainsworth, Bell, and Stayton (1971) classified them into three groups on the basis of responses to reunion with the mother. The first group was active in seeking proximity to and interaction with the mother upon reunion. This group was norma-tive—it contained the greatest number of infants and also epito-mized the predicted theoretical model of secure attachment. A second group sought relatively little proximity to or interaction with the mother, but actively avoided her upon reunion. A third group mixed seeking of proximity and contact with resistance of contact and interaction. Ainsworth and her associates found relationships between the infant's strange-situation behavior and his home behavior, and between his behavior and maternal behavior in the home. Infants in the first group had histories of harmonious, secure interaction with mothers who were sensitive to their signals for contact and interaction. Infants in the other two groups had histories of disharmonious, insecure interaction with insensitive mothers. On the basis of these findings, Ainsworth concluded that a child's responses to separation from and reunion with his mother in the strange situation provided an accurate picture of the quality of their interaction. The strange situation was, in effect, a convenient, short-hand way of assessing some significant qualitative aspects of attachment relationships.

Although Ainsworth had used her situation to study individual differences in attachment relationships, others (Maccoby & Feldman 1972; Marvin 1971) have also used the technique to observe normative patterns of attachment behavior and changes in these patterns over the first four years of life. They found a gradual decline in seeking contact with the mother upon reunion and then in seeking proximity to her. Maintaining contact to the mother upon reunion tended to disappear by age two and seeking of proximity by age four. Separation protest declined more sharply around age three.

In the present study, the strange situation was used to compare responses to separation from and reunion with the mother in groups of day-care and home-reared children. Three alternative hypotheses were offered about the comparisons: (1) day-care children would behave no differently from home-reared children, on the assumption that day care had not affected attachment; (2) day-care children would be less distressed by separation and would exhibit correspondingly less intensely heightened attachment behaviors upon reunion because of their more frequent experiences with separation; (3) day-care children would exhibit disturbances in attachment related to daily separation; and the type of disturbance would be related to the child's developmental level at the time of entering day care.

SUBJECTS

The subjects were forty middle-class children, all but one white. Twenty were enrolled in full-time group day-care and twenty were reared by their mothers at home. Ten of the day-care group had entered centers at a mean age of 25.66 months (SD=1.81 months) and ten at a mean age of 34.88 months (SD=2.45 months). Both groups had been enrolled for approximately the same length of time when observed—4.55 months for the younger group (SD=2.56 months) and 4.78 months for the older group (SD=1.69 months). When observed they had mean ages of 30.23 months (SD=2.20 months) and 39.62 months (SD=1.98 months) respectively. The mean ages of the home-reared groups at the time of observation were 30.23 months (SD=1.98 months) and 39.46 months (SD=1.95 months). Equal numbers of males and females were observed at each age level.

One assumption underlying the comparison was that the groups were equivalent on variables affecting the quality of attachment other than the daily separations implicit in day-care. This assumption would be unnecessary in an experimental study which randomly assigned children to day care or home rearing, but such a study would obviously be extremely difficult to carry out. The children were from middle-class homes, both in terms of parental education and income. Both parents were present in the home. Measures of the home environment (reported below) were also taken as a first part of the study, and they support this assumption of equivalence between the groups. Eighty percent of day-care children and sixty percent of home-reared children were firstborns. Four day-care children had been cared for by baby-sitters approximately four months before starting group day care. Three home-reared forty-month-olds attended nursery school two or three mornings a week.

Cooperation in collecting a day-care sample was obtained from four private centers that followed traditional nursery school regimes with relatively little emphasis on structured preschool academic programs. The degrees of structuring in play and the amount of organized group activities were greater for the older children than for the younger. Children were segregated into groups of two- and three-year-olds, four-year-olds, and five-year-olds. Two care-givers were assigned to each group, and they did not shift over the course of the week. On the average, care-givers tended to remain in their positions for three years. At age four, and again at age five, children moved up into a new group with new care-givers. In the two- and three-year-old group, the ratio of care-givers to children was 1:8 or 1:6, depending on the center. Names of all children attending the center were provided beforehand by the directors, and from this list parents were contacted individually. All but one agreed to cooperate. Pediatricians in private practice supplied names of home-reared children, and all but two parents contacted agreed to participate.

DATA-COLLECTION PROCEDURES

The first part of the procedure involved a home visit of an hour and a half duration to each mother-child pair. Its purposes were to establish rapport with the mother, to instruct her about the study, and to assess the general quality of stimulation provided the child by his home environment. The mother was asked to have her child present during part of the visit so that mother-child interaction could be observed, and she was also interviewed about her child-care practices. Following the visit, each mother was rated on an "empathy" scale (devised by Hogan 1969) and on the Caldwell Inventory of Home Stimulation (1970). The empathy scale was used to investigate possible differences between mothers in sensitivity to social signals—a variable which Ainsworth and associates (Ainsworth, Bell, & Stayton 1971) have suggested is an important determinant of the quality of infant-mother attachment. The Caldwell Inventory is a straightforward tool which depends primarily on first-hand observation of the physical aspects of the home (such as number and type of toys the child had) and on observation of mother-child interaction, rather than on maternal report alone. For example, it was noted if the mother spoke spontaneously to the child, if she caressed or kissed him, if books were present and visible, or if he had a pet. Subscales dealt with the mother's emotional-verbal responsiveness, avoidance of restriction and punishment, involvement with the child, provision of appropriate play materials, organization of his physical and temporal environments, and the opportunities he had for variety in daily stimulation.

Within two weeks after the home visit, each mother-child pair came to The Johns Hopkins University for the strange situation. It consists of eight episodes, each, except for the first, three minutes long. These are shown in Table 1.1.

The situation was used to observe systematically the child's use of his mother as a base from which to explore, his responses to a

Table 1.1. Strange Situation Episodes

Episode no.	Duration	Participants	Description of episode
1	30 sec, approx.	Observer, mother, child	Observer ushers mother and child into the room. Child is set down on floor.
2	3 min	Mother, child	Child is free to explore. M reads a magazine.
3	3 min	Stranger, mother, child	Stranger enters, sits quietly for a moment, interacts with mother, then with child.
4	3 min*	Stranger, child	M leaves. Stranger remains with child; responds to his advances or comforts him if necessary.
5	3 min	Mother, child	Stranger leaves as mother enters. Mother comforts child if he is distressed, then reinterests him in toys.
6	3 min*	Child	Mother leaves child alone in room.
7	3 min*	Stranger, child	Stranger enters; attempts to comfort child if distressed; returns to her chair.
8	3 min	Mother, child	Mother enters as stranger leaves. Mother behaves as in episode 5.

*The duration of episode was curtailed if the child became very distressed.

stranger, and to brief separation from and reunion with the mother in an unfamiliar environment. It took place in a pleasantly furnished room which contained toys for the child to play with and chairs for the mother and stranger. The first three episodes of the situation were preseparation episodes and were relatively nonstressful. Episode 1 was introductory. Episode 2 was intended to elicit exploratory behaviors. The first possible stress was introduced in Episode 3 with the stranger's entrance. Episode 4, the first separation, began with the mother's unobtrusive departure. If the child continued to play, then the stranger was nonparticipant; otherwise, she attempted to engage his interest in the toys. If the child became distressed, she tried to distract him and, if this failed, then the episode was terminated before three minutes had elapsed. Episode 5 was the first reunion. The mother paused in the door to give the child an opportunity to mobilize a spontaneous response, since the focus of this and the subsequent reunion episode was on the degree to which attachment behaviors had been heightened by separation. In Episode 6, the mother left the room, pausing to say, "Bye-bye, I'll be back." In Episode 7, the stranger returned and behaved as previously. Episode 8 involved another reunion with the mother.

Meanwhile, the behavior of the children was observed from an adjoining room through a one-way vision window. A continuous description of events was dictated into recorders, which also picked up the sound of a buzzer every fifteen seconds. The transcribed narrative reports were marked off into these time intervals for analysis. In 65 percent of cases, there were two independent observers, and in the other cases the investigator served as sole observer. The second observer in all but four instances was unaware of the hypotheses of the study or the child's rearing group membership. Two women played the role of stranger for all but three of the children.

MEASURES

The individual accounts of the children's behavior were consolidated for analysis and three types of measures were extracted: frequency measures, percentage measures, and scores of social interaction with the mother and the stranger.

Frequency Measures

Four measures were obtained by making counts of the number of 15-second intervals in which the following behaviors occurred: exploratory manipulation of the toys, crying and oral behavior —sucking of thumb or chewing or sucking on toys. Another frequency measure was a composite of the individual frequencies of speaking to the mother, smiling at her, and showing her a toy. This measure (labeled "distance interaction") was obtained only in Episode 2, when the mother and child were alone together and when the mother was noninterventive, in order to obtain an index of the child's spontaneous interest in her. In Episode 3, the presence of the stranger reduced this behavior to virtually zero. Coefficients of interobserver reliability were obtained and were all quite good: exploratory manipulation, .98; oral behavior, .90; distance interaction, .85; and crying, .98.

Social Interaction Scores

Another part of the analysis involved detailed codings of socially interactive behaviors with the mother and with the stranger on the basis of narrative reports. Each child was scored on the intensity of seeking proximity, of avoiding proximity and interaction and of resisting contact and interaction. A measure of the intensity of his search for the mother during separation episodes was also obtained. This scoring system was originally devised by Ainsworth, Bell, and Stayton (1971) for use with one-year-olds, and was revised by Marvin (1971) for use with two-, three-, and four-year-olds. Each behavior was assessed on a seven-point scale which took into account contingencies of adult behavior as well as contingencies of child behavior.

The following is a brief description of the behavioral contents of each scale.

Proximity and Contact-Seeking. This variable deals with the child's attempts to gain proximity to the adult. High scores are given to active full approaches ending in physical contact, and low ones to relatively passive behaviors which indicate a desire for contact, such as leaning toward the adult's out-stretched arms.

Proximity and Interaction-Avoiding. This variable deals with active avoidance behaviors. In the case of the mother, such behavior is only identifiable with accuracy after separations, when approach and/or distance greeting are the norm. In the case of a stranger, avoidance is identifiable in those situations in which a child could easily interact with her or merely accept her presence. High scores are given to prolonged gaze aversion, physical withdrawal; and attempts to leave the room (in the case of the mother); intermediate scores are given to such behaviors as clear-cut looking away; and low scores are given to brief gaze aversion, or other very slight instances of avoidance.

Resisting. This variable deals with the child's attempts to openly reject contact or interaction. High scores are given to strong physical rejection of the adult's attempts to pick up the child or to intervene in his activities; intermediate ones to fairly isolated instances of clearly resistant behaviors, such as throwing of a toy the adult has offered; and low scores to behaviors such as a protest upon seeing the adult approach. Unlike avoidance, resistance has an overtly angry quality to it.

Search Behavior. This variable deals with the child's attempts to regain proximity to his mother during separation episodes. High scores are given to active attempts to open the door; intermediate ones to behaviors, such as trips to the mother's chair; and low scores to such behaviors as a brief glance at the door.

Each child was scored on the scales by two independent judges, one of whom was unaware of the child's rearing-group classification. All coefficients of reliability were .90 or higher.

RESULTS

The Home Visit

There were no significant differences between mothers in the day-care and home-care groups on the measure of interpersonal empathy or on the Caldwell Inventory of Home Stimulation. While it was not possible to make detailed assessments of individual patterns of mother-child interaction in the home or differences in maternal sensitivity to the child, the findings do suggest that, at least broadly, children in both groups were receiving similar care and that their home environments were adequate to promote healthy development.

A Comparison of the Behavior of Day-Care and Home-Care Children in the Strange Situation

In the analysis of the data on strange situation behavior, possible differences between children in the two rearing situations were examined, as were possible interactions between method of care and the child's age. The latter analyses were of importance because of a theoretical interest in the effects of day care on children of different ages. The findings will be presented in four parts dealing with play behaviors in the strange situation, children's responses to separation, their patterns of social interaction with the mother, and their reaction to the stranger who was present in three episodes of the situation.

Play

Play behaviors in the strange situation typically consisted of manipulation of toys present in the room on and about the child's chair and occasionally in exploration of some other object in the room—a cabinet for instance. There was a significant age X rearing group interaction in total amount of play $F(1, 32) = 6.93$, $p < .025$. Day-care forty-month-olds were lowest in amount of play throughout the strange situation ($X = 7.48$), whereas home-reared forty-month-olds were highest ($X = 9.68$). Day-care thirty-month-olds were intermediate between their home-care age counterparts ($X = 8.9$ versus $X = 8.2$) and the older home-care children. All groups decreased in amount of exploration during separation episodes, but these changes were most pronounced in the older day-care group and least pronounced in the older home-care group.

Separation Behaviors

Included in this analysis were behaviors classically considered indicators of separation anxiety—namely, the amount of crying a child does, the amount of oral behavior in which he engages, and the intensity of his attempts to regain proximity to his absent mother.

Day-care children were significantly more likely to cry throughout the strange situation than home-care children $F(1,32) = 4.60$, $p < .05$. But an interaction of age X rearing method, $F(1,32) = 3.78$, $p < .07$, suggested that the rearing-group difference was accounted for chiefly by differences in the amount of crying between day-care and home-care forty-month-olds. The older day-care children cried an average of 3.3 intervals per episode, whereas the older home-care children cried almost not at all—.22 of one 15-second interval. The differences between the younger children in the two rearing groups were much less, but the day-care children tended to cry more than home-care children ($X = 1.72$ versus $X = 1.57$).

Oral behavior was also more likely to occur in the day-care group than in the home-care group (randomization test for two independent samples: $p < .005$), although in this case there was no difference between children of different ages. Orality occurred most often in Episode 7, when the stranger reentered the room after the child had been alone during a second separation. The presence of orality in this episode apparently resulted both from anxiety over the mother's whereabouts and from apprehension over the appearance of the stranger when the child was expecting his mother to walk through the door.

Search for the mother was shown most strongly by day-care forty-month-olds ($X = 3.72$) and by home-care thirty-month-olds ($X = 3.72$); and least strongly by the older home-care children ($X = 2.05$) and younger day-care children ($X = 2.75$). This interaction of rearing method and age of child $F(1,32) = 5.14$, $p < .05$) is depicted in Figure 1.1.

The older day-care children were particularly conspicuous for their active search behavior in Episode 4, the first separation, when children in the other groups tended to maintain exploratory behavior or perhaps merely looked at the door or mother's chair, if they displayed search behavior at all.

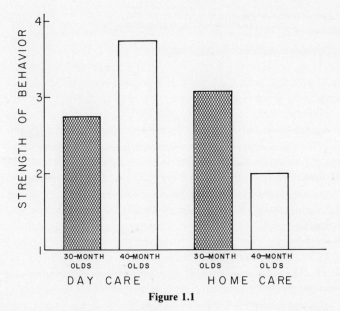

Figure 1.1

BEHAVIOR TO THE MOTHER

Distance Interaction

Even before separation had occurred and before the stranger had entered the room to introduce even a mild source of stress, day care children differed in the amount of distance interaction they engaged in with their mothers $F(1,32) = 6.66$, $p < .05$. Distance interaction commonly occurred in the course of exploratory activities. Typically, the child might pause briefly and show his mother a toy, or perhaps ask her permission to play with it. By itself, the finding of a difference between children in the two groups on this variable is equivocal. It could be interpreted as indicating that day-care children are more independent of their mothers in free-play activities, perhaps because of their daily experiences of playing without the mother. However, a negative correlation ($r = -.42$, $p < .01$) was found between distance interaction and resistant and avoidant behaviors in the reunion episodes. This suggests that relatively little interaction with the mother under nonstressful conditions may indicate a qualitative disturbance in their relationship, which becomes more apparent after a separation has clearly heightened attachment behaviors.

Proximity-Seeking Behaviors

A child's tendency to seek proximity to his mother is commonly held to be the hallmark of his attachment to her. Especially after a separation experience, individual differences in this tendency are highlighted (Ainsworth 1973). Figure 1.2 shows that day-care and home-care children did not differ in the amount of proximity they sought to their mothers in Episodes 2 or 3, before separation. Differences emerge, however, in the reunion episodes, Episodes 5 and 8 (age X rearing group X episode interaction: $F(1,32) = 3.85$, $p < .025$). In Episode 5 day-care forty-month-olds show heightened attachment behavior relative to their home-care counterparts. In Episode 8, the older day-care children continue to increase in proximity-seeking and the older home-care children decline slightly. Home-care thirty-month-olds show a clear heightening of proxim-

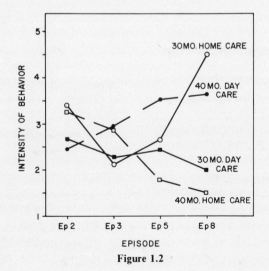

Figure 1.2

ity-seeking in this episode, but their day-care counterparts tend to decline.

Resisting and Avoiding Behaviors

Resistant behaviors occurred relatively infrequently, perhaps because mothers did not often try to pick the child up or to interfere with his ongoing activities. The resistant behavior which did occur most often took the form of displays of temper, especially when the mother tried to confine the child or restrict his activities. Resistant behaviors of some type were observed in six out of ten of the older day-care children, and in two of the younger children. They were also observed in two home-care thirty-month-olds, but in none of the older home-care children. Taken in conjunction with the relatively high amount of proximity-seeking to the mother, the occurrence of resistance in the older day-care children suggests ambivalence.

As seen in Figure 1.3, proximity and interaction avoidant behaviors were more conspicuous in day-care children of both ages than in home-care children $F(1,32) = 16.36$, $p < .005$.

Responses to the Stranger

While the major focus of the strange situation comparison between day-care and home-care children was on attachment behaviors, the presence of the stranger in three episodes provided an opportunity to examine the children's reaction to her. Day-care children were more avoidant of the stranger than home-care children $F(1,32) = 13.26$, $p < .001$, and their aversion to her increased during separations. In contrast, home-care children were most apprehensive about the stranger when she initially entered the room in Episode 3 (mother, child, stranger) and became less so in subsequent separation episodes (rearing group X episode interaction, $F(1,32) = 4.30$, $p < .05$). Day-care forty-month-olds tended to be more resistant of the stranger, especially during separation

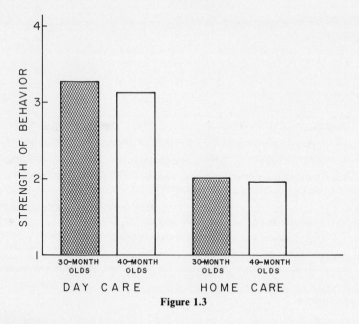

Figure 1.3

episodes, than the other children (age X rearing-group interaction: $F(1,32) = 4.30$, $p < .05$).

CONCLUSIONS AND DISCUSSION

Summary of Findings

Relative to home-care children, day-care children exhibited patterns of behavior in the strange situation which can be interpreted as indicating a disturbance in attachment. Before separation they interacted across a distance with the mother significantly less than the home-care children. During separations they exhibited more distress and orality, and upon reunion they were more avoidant of the mother. Likewise, they were more avoidant of the stranger.

Despite these similarities between both age groups of day-care children, they were different from each other and from their respective home-care controls in some important ways.

First of all, in the day-care groups themselves there occurred a "reversal" of developmental trends in attachment behavior found both in the home-care groups and also in studies reported elsewhere (e.g., Marvin 1971; Maccoby & Feldman 1972). It was the younger day-care children who were less likely to search for their mothers during separation or to protest their absences rather than the older children. Younger day-care children also were less likely to seek proximity to the mother upon reunion. In general, their exploratory behaviors were more robust than those of the older day-care group. In the home-care groups, opposite age trends were found.

Second, in comparison to home-care children of the same age, children who started day-care at approximately twenty-five months of age sought relatively little proximity to the mother upon reunion, but also actively avoided her. In comparison to the older home-care children, children who started day-care at approximately thirty-five months of age were more anxious throughout the strange situation. They also sought more proximity to the mother upon reunion but mixed these approaches with resistant and avoidant behaviors.

The strange situation clearly had an age-differential effect. It heightened proximity and interaction avoidant tendencies in the younger day-care children and anxious ambivalent tendencies in older day-care children.

These findings are congruent with those of Robertson and Bowlby (1952) on children's responses to separations. In their sample, it was the younger children—between one and two-and-a-half years of age—who were more likely to exhibit detachment behaviors than the older children who were likely to exhibit anxious attachment behaviors. Recently Ainsworth (1973) has reported that the repetition of minor strange situations at a two-week interval sensitizes rather than habituates one-year-olds. These findings lend credence to the notion that the behaviors of the day-care children in the present study may stem from the experience of repeated daily mother-child separation.

However, there are certain qualifications which must be made. First, reference to "classic" separation studies in interpreting the present data does not imply that day-care children are seriously harmed by day-care separation, as are children by long institutional separation. However, to the extent that there exists prototypical separation response which children display in a range of separation situations, the findings do suggest the daily separations in group day-care may also disturb the quality of child's attachment to his mother.

Anxious attachment and detachment are both thought to stem from the same source (major separation), but detachment is the more alarming symptom because it implies that a child is cut off from close interpersonal relationships. Anxious attachment, even if it is of an ambivalent nature, does not preclude the maintenance of a close mother-child relationship. However, in the case of the present day-care children, it is not clear what the anxious and avoidant behaviors signify for mother-child interaction. However, the avoidant behaviors of the younger children may possibly signal a more substantial disruption of the mother-child relationship than the anxious attachment of the older children, although at first glance it is the younger day-care children who appear less overtly disturbed.

In order to ascertain the significance for development of the reactions observed in the present day-care sample, several questions must be answered. First, do the equations which relate strange situation behaviors to pervasive qualitative differences in infant-mother attachment in one-year-olds hold also for two- and three-year-olds? What are the long-term implications of reactions observed in the strange situation? What is needed in order to answer these questions are further home observations of day-care and home-care children, as well as further observations of children several years after day-care.

It may also be asked to what extent the results of the present study can be attributed to day-care separations rather than to differences in mother-child interaction that were already present prior to the day-care experience. This interpretative difficulty could be circumvented in a study in which children were randomly assigned to day-care or home-rearing, but most mothers will not allow their decision to stay at home with their children or to place them in substitute care to be dictated by the demands of a research design. In the past, the strange situation has been used to reflect individual differences in infant-mother interaction that were related to differences in maternal behavior (Ainsworth, Bell, & Stayton 1971), but others (e.g., Maccoby & Feldman 1972) have used it to compare groups of children with different rearing histories. However, in the present study, strange situation behavior may also reflect differences in mother-child interaction established before the day-care experience was introduced in the one group. There is no evidence that the mothers of the present sample of day-care children were different from the stay-at-home mothers, as they were assessed on the Caldwell Inventory and the Hogan Empathy scale. However, Hoffman (1974) finds attitudinal differences between working mothers and unemployed mothers, although she has not been able to examine large samples of mothers who work when their children are of preschool age. Moore's evidence suggests that the mother's personality and, hence, presumably her care-giving practices can interact with such variables as the child's age and the quality and stability of substitute care in determining his long-term reaction to such care (Moore 1964, 1969). Hence, it is possible that the mothers of the present day-care children differed from mothers of home-reared children on dimensions which were not tapped by the home measures obtained and which either could have caused the results, or could have interacted with the day-care experience to cause the behaviors observed in the strange situation.

Comparison with Other Studies of Day-Care and Attachment

The results of the present study are at variance with those of Caldwell et al., who reported essentially no differences between day-care and home-care children on a number of variables relating to strength of attachment. There are a number of factors which may account for this. First, the infants at the Caldwell Child Center may have received care which was so individualized that it was the equivalent in quality of maternal care. If this was so, then a relationship with the care-giver, who would also function as an attachment figure, would probably compensate for any adverse reaction to separation from the mother.

Related to this is the possibility that children who are used to group care from infancy might not exhibit the same patterns of disruption in the attachment to the mother as children who are suddenly shifted from home-care to day-care after a longer period of time during which the relationship to the mother has been consoli-

dated and intensified. This possibility receives at least some anec-
dotal support from the day-care study by Kearsley et al. (in press).
They found that infants who started in their nursery school at 3 1/2
months adjusted considerably better than infants who started only
two months later. In this two-month period, most infants would be
forming at least a rudimentary attachment to the mother. They also
reported that children who were absent from the nursery for more
than a week showed evidence of distress when they returned. Two
13 1/2-month-olds they attempted to enroll refused to eat and
fretted so persistently that they were forced to discontinue their
participation. Hence, there is some reason to believe that the child's
age is a major influence on his reaction to day-care separation.

It must be pointed out that Caldwell was concerned chiefly with
measuring intensity of attachment in children younger than those in
the present sample. In the present study, since it was the younger
day-care children who sought relatively little proximity, and the
older day-care children who sought relatively much; and since the
opposite trend was true in the home-care groups, day-care and
home-care children would have appeared equally intensely attached,
had age differences not been taken into account. Also, the present
study highlighted resistant and avoidant behaviors as indicators of
qualitative aspects of the attachment relationship. An absence of
much proximity-seeking to the mother in reunion, coupled with
avoidance, is taken to indicate a defensive reaction rather than weak
attachment. In general, a failure to attend to the relationships
among proximity-seeking behaviors, crying, and negative features
of the child's interaction with his mother, and a tendency to focus on
strength of attachment, may well obscure findings which depend on
configurational analyses.

An Examination of Some Arguments in Favor of Group Day-Care

At this point it is well to review some arguments commonly
used in favor of group day-care with the findings of the present
study in mind. The first, and perhaps among the most compelling
argument in its favor, is that day-care is beneficial to children who
might otherwise suffer declines in cognitive development if they

were to continue being reared in environmentally depriving homes. There is some evidence that high-quality day-care programs can prevent these declines (e.g., Caldwell et al. 1970; Keister 1971), although alternatives, such as training the mother in the home rather than removing the child from her, are also being investigated (Gordon 1970). In general, maternal involvement seems a critical factor in maintaining any gains produced by such programs. All things considered, benefits that disadvantaged children gain in developmental centers would seem to weigh heavily in favor of day-care for them, provided that such care also has no detrimental effects on their social development.

Another pressing argument in favor of day-care is that some mothers must work and have to choose between a day-care center or erratic care available in their neighborhoods. If the neighborhood care is indeed erratic and the day-care stable and stimulating, then it would seem preferable. However, more studies are needed to compare the effects of typical baby-sitting arrangements, family day-care, and group day-care on young children.

In the case of children whose home environments are adequately supportive of development, there is as yet little evidence that group day-care will provide the child with long-term cognitive advantages relative to the home-reared child. And there is no evidence that group day-care has enduring beneficial effects on social development relative to home care. The very best day-care centers continue to try and simulate home-care by providing low child:adult ratios. Unfortunately, the financial cost in such cases is very high, and many day-care programs today fall short of optimal conditions.

Another argument commonly advanced in favor of day-care is that children are better off away from mothers who are unhappy with a full-time maternal role. The amount of psychological discontent among women who unwillingly stay at home with young children is increasing as societal supports for the role of full-time mother are disappearing. These women may unwittingly create more strain in their relationships with their children than women who are more satisfied with their position in the home. One practical solution to this problem is to enroll the child in a day-care center where hopefully he can establish satisfactory relationships with substitute care-givers and with peers. Especially if the mother's own care has been erratic, stable substitute care may be of some benefit to children. However, it is also possible that children who enter day-care as a result of implicit maternal rejection or unsatisfactory relationships may react to the separation more adversely than those whose mothers enroll them for other reasons. Two studies (Jessner, Blom, & Waldfogel 1952; Prugh, Staub, Sands, Kirschbaum, & Lenihan 1953) established a relationship between maternal irritability and disproportionately severe, enduring reactions to separation. Likewise, it is possible that children who enter group-care as a consequence of parental separation may already feel more insecure than children from maritally intact families. Enrollment in day-care (especially if it follows immediately upon a family break-up) may exacerbate their anxiety. Hence, it is necessary to weigh the advantages which may accrue to emotionally "high-risk" children from group day-care against possible further disruption of the child's relationship with his mother and family.

It is also commonly argued that group day-care will promote healthy independence of the mother and will correct any overdependence resulting from "too exclusive" an attachment to mother.

Some people have equated security of attachment with strong dependency behaviors. However, Ainsworth (1973) has presented evidence that children who display the greatest amount of anxious crying in the home are insecure in their relationships with the mother rather than "too attached." She further states that attachment and independence are not necessarily opposed, since a secure relationship with the mother provides the child with the confidence he needs to explore both his physical and social environments. As the child grows, physical distancing between himself and his mother normally will increase, but it can be hampered by maternal rejection or inaccessibility which heighten attachment behaviors at the expense of exploratory behaviors. The findings of the present study suggest that *physical* inaccessibility which daily separation implies may also impede the growth of independence. In the strange situation, it was the home-reared forty-month-olds who showed the greatest degree of independence from the mother, but their independence did not preclude their keeping in touch with the mother across a distance. On the other hand, day-care forty-month-olds were least independent. While the younger day-care group appeared to be more independent than their home-reared age controls on the measure of proximity-seeking, their proximity and interaction avoiding tendencies suggest that their relative independence may be at the expense of their relationship with the mother.

It is also commonly assumed that day-care, like nursery school, will make a child better able to affiliate with new people. While it is true that a child reared exclusively by his mother will, like Harlow's isolate monkeys, probably be at a social disadvantage relative to those with exposure to peers, it is not clear that day-care will bestow an advantage in affiliative ability relative to normal home-care in which a child receives daily exposure to other children in his neighborhood and, perhaps, nursery school experience. The findings of the present study indicated greater avoidance of a stranger in day-care children in comparison to their home-care controls. While this finding makes no sense in terms of a social exposure theory, it is consistent with findings (Tizard & Tizard 1971; Heinicke & Westheimer 1965) that children who were separated from their mothers in residential nurseries were more fearful of strangers than home-reared children. In the present study, it is possible that day-care children were only reacting to the stranger's presence in an unfamiliar environment as a cue that the mother was going to leave them. Under other circumstances, they may respond to adults much as home-reared children. Or there may be a more general relationship between the anxiety versus security that a child experiences in his primary attachment relationship and the anxiety versus security he demonstrates in interacting with unfamiliar figures.

More recently, Schwarz et al. (Schwarz, Krolick, & Strickland 1973; Schwarz, Strickland, & Krolick 1974) reported that prior day-care experience facilitates entrance into a new day-care center; but also that children who started day-care as infants were significantly more aggressive, more motorically active, and less cooperative with adults, than children who began at age three or four. He suggests that early day-care experience may slow acquisition of adult cultural values. The issue of day-care's effect on affiliative and dependency behaviors to other children and adults appears quite complex and in need of further research.

Finally, many have attacked the ethnocentrism implicit in taking the nuclear family as more "natural" to children than day-care. They have argued that a number of different types of child care have been proven successful in other societies and that day-care is viable in American society. Frequent reference is made to extended family arrangements, kibbutz rearing and Soviet, Eastern European, and Chinese day-care. However, the extended family, unlike group day-care, provides the child not only with care from his mother and relatives who are more or less permanent family members but also with children of various ages. The setting is familiar to him and he is not separated from his own mother. While high-quality day-care may provide children with a network of social relationships in the center, it is unlikely that such relationships will be of the same degree of stability and intimacy as those found in the extended family.

Also, there is as yet no rigorous way of making systematic comparisons of American day-care with day-care in other societies, chiefly because of the lack of psychologically oriented research. Day-care is probably a different type of experience for a child from a small village or a closely knit community than it is for a child from a more impersonal urban environment. Gewirtz (1971) has cautioned against generalizations from Israeli kibbutzim and American day care because of differences in community life styles, physical settings, and ideological commitments of individuals involved in the care.

SUMMARY

It must be stressed that, at the present time, no one piece of research can stand as any more than suggestive of possible outcomes of group day-care on children from clearly defined experiential backgrounds, social classes, and ages who are enrolled in specific types of day-care. Hopefully, many works taken together may yield more detailed knowledge about the desirability of a particular type of substitute care for an individual child. It may be that family day-care arrangements, where a child is attended by a substitute mother figure usually in her own home, or part-time group-care are more suited to the needs of young children under age three or four than typical full-time group-care. While some maternal care enthusiasts have proposed paying women to stay at home with their children, this does not allow for the fact that some mothers desire to work. Hence, alternatives to both full-time maternal care and full-time group day-care must be explored.

Within the framework of group day-care, the effects of regimes that vary in practices for introducing children to the center and in specific types of child-care practices must also be investigated in order to see if some are more effective than others in reducing separation-related disturbances. To the extent that specific practices can do so, then they will also probably reduce or eliminate possible negative influences in the mother-child relationship. Research attention must also be devoted to the issue of importance of continuity of care in the day-care center. That is, how critical is it that young children, particularly those who enroll in day-care as infants while they are forming their first attachments, have relatively continuous care from one specific figure in the center as well as from their mothers at home? Will shifts of care-givers to whom the young child is likely to form attachments result in discernible increases in anxiety? If continuity in substitute care-giving proves to be important for the social development of young children in substitute care, then the problem of motivating care-givers to remain in their positions arises. At present there is a high turnover of day-care staff because of the relatively low salary and status associated with the jobs.

In a practical sense, it may be that the requirements of young children for continuous intimate relationships with a stable mother figure may be difficult to reconcile with the desires of young women for freedom to devote themselves to full-time employment outside the home. Bowlby's attachment theory sounds a cautionary note when we contemplate far-reaching changes in child care that deviate too dramatically from continuous one-to-one relationships. However, the options which parents have for their child's care are influenced by and limited by social trends. In today's world, with its almost constant changes and increasing instability, it is becoming difficult for parents to rear their children as they themselves were reared, even if they desired to do so. It is considered nostalgic to pine for child-care patterns which were prevalent in the United States some ten or twenty years ago. A revival of the extended family would be considered desirable by most people; but this may be difficult to achieve in urban environments. It has been proposed that father and mother.both work part-time and hence share child-care responsibilities, so that the child is in daily contact with an enduring attachment figure. Such a proposal also has great appeal, but again it may prove to be difficult to accomplish on a large scale, unless the entire structure of employment and the demands of well-paying jobs are radically changed.

The developing trend toward smaller families and decreases in social pressure on young couples to have children at all may lead to some relief to the present child-care dilemma. Couples who have children in the near future may do so with a commitment to spend a substantial proportion of their adult lives rearing them personally, while other couples are free to pursue other activities without suffering from guilt feelings for not having children. The area of child-care practices is an emotional one, in which research is inevitably undertaken within a broader social and political context. Emotional reactions to research findings are to be expected, but they should not be allowed to impede progress toward a rational definition of optimal environments for rearing children. True, society is changing and child-care practices must accommodate, but society must accommodate even more to the requirements of young children for healthy development, if it is to protect its most valuable human resource.

REFERENCES

Ainsworth, M. D. S. 1973. The development of infant-mother attachment. In B. M. Caldwell and H. N. Ricciuti (eds.), *Review of child development research:* vol. 3. Chicago: University of Chicago Press.

————. Anxious attachment and defensive reactions in a strange situation and their relationship to behavior at home. Paper presented at the biennial meeting of the Society for Research in Child Development, Philadelphia, March 1973.

Ainsworth, M. D. S., & Bell, S. M. 1970. Attachment, exploration, and separation: Illustrated by the behavior of one-year-olds in a strange situation. *Child Development* 41: 4–67.

Ainsworth, M. D. S., Bell, S. M., & Stayton, D. J. 1971. Individual differences in strange-situation behavior of one-year-olds. In H. R.

Schaffer (ed.), *The origins of human social relations.* London: Academic Press.

Ainsworth, M. D. S., & Wittig, B. A. 1969. Attachment and exploratory behavior of one-year-olds in a strange situation. In B. M. Foss (ed.), *Determinants of infant behavior IV.* London: Methuen, pp. 111–36.

Bender, L., & Yarnell, H. 1941. An observation nursery: A study of 250 children in the psychiatric division of Bellevue Hospital. *American Journal of Psychiatry* 97: 1158.

Blehar, M. C. 1974. Anxious attachment and defensive reactions associated with day care. *Child Development* 45: 683–92.

Bowlby, J. 1969. *Attachment and loss.* vol. I: *Attachment.* London: Hogarth; New York: Basic Books.

────── 1973. *Attachment and loss.* vol. II: *Separation.* London: Hogarth.

Caldwell, B. M., Wright, C., Honig, A. S., & Tannenbaum, J. 1970. Infant day care and attachment. *American Journal of Orthopsychiatry* 40: 397–412.

Gewirtz, H. 1971. Child care facilities and "The Israeli Experience." In *Day care: Resources for decisions.* E. Grotberg (ed.), Office of Economic Opportunity, Office of Planning, Research, and Evaluation, pp. 38–49.

Goldfarb, W. 1943. The effects of early institutional care on adolescent personality. *Child Development* 14: 441.

Gordon, I. J. 1970. Reaching the young child through parent education. *Childhood Education* 4: 247–49.

Heinicke, C. M., & Westheimer, I. 1965. *Brief separations.* New York: International Universities Press.

Hoffman, Lois. 1974. Effects of maternal employment on the child: A review of research. *Developmental Psychology* 10(2): 204–28.

Hoffman, R., & Stolz, L. M. 1961. Changes in family functioning as intermediary effects of maternal employment. In A. Siegal (ed.), *Research issues related to the effects of maternal employment on children.* Pennsylvania State University.

Hogan, R. 1969. Development of an empathy scale. *Journal of Consulting and Clinical Psychology* 33(5): 307–16.

Jessner, L. M., Blom, G., & Waldfogel, S. 1952. Emotional implications of tonsillectomy and adenoidectomy on children. In *Psychoanalytic study of the child.* New York: International Universities Press.

Kearsley, R. B., Zelazo, P. R., Kagan, J. I., & Hartmann, R. Separation protest in day-care and home-reared infants. *Pediatrics* (in press).

Keister, M. E. 1972. "The Good Life" for infants and toddlers. Washington, D.C.: National Association for the Education of Young Children.

Maccoby, E., & Feldman, S. 1972. Mother-attachment and stranger reactions. *Monographs of the Society for Research in Child Development* 37: 146.

Marvin, R. 1971. Attachment and communicative behavior in two, three and four year old children. Doctoral dissertation, University of Chicago.

Moore, T. 1964. Children of full-time and part-time mothers. *International Journal of Social Psychiatry* 2: 1–10.

———. 1969. Stress in normal childhood. *Human Relations* 22: 235–50.

Provence, S., & Lipton, R. C. 1962. *Infants in institutions.* New York: International Universities Press.

Prugh, D. G., Staub, E. M., Sands, H., Kirschbaum, R. M., & Lenihan, E. A. 1953. A study of the emotional reactions of children and families to hospitalization and illness. *American Journal of Orthopsychiatry* 23: 70.

Robertson, J., & Bowlby, J. 1952. Responses of young children to separation from their mothers. Courrier: Centre internationale de l'enfance 2: 131–42.

Robertson, J., & Robertson, J. 1971. *Young children in brief separations.* New York: Quadrangle.

Schwarz, J. C., Krolick, G., & Strickland, R. 1973. Effects of early day care experience on adjustment to a new environment. *American Journal of Orthopsychiatry* 43(3): 340–46.

Schwarz, J. C., Strickland, R., & Krolick, R. G. 1974. Infant day care: Behavioral effects at preschool age. *Developmental Psychology* 19: 502–06.

Tizard, J., & Tizard, B. 1971. The social development of two-year-old children in residential nurseries. In H. R. Schaffer (ed.), *The origins of human social relations.* London: Academic Press.

Yarrow, L. J. 1961. Maternal deprivation: Toward an empirical and conceptual evaluation. *Psychological Bulletin* 58: 459–90.

2

ANALYSIS OF A PECULIAR FORM OF REUNION BEHAVIOR SEEN IN SOME DAY-CARE CHILDREN: ITS HISTORY AND SEQUELAE IN CHILDREN WHO ARE HOME-REARED

Mary B. Main

I saw the first symptoms of shyness in my child when nearly two years and three months old; this was shown towards myself after an absence of ten days from home, chiefly by his eyes being kept slightly averted from mine; but he soon came and sat on my knee and kissed me, and all trace of shyness disappeared.

Darwin, 1877

In the context of reunion following brief separations in a strange environment, most year-old infants seek proximity and even contact with their mothers: as behavior this is expectable and as fact it is well documented. In this same context, however, some infants avoid their mothers, looking away, turning away, moving away, or ignoring them altogether. While avoidance of primary attachment figures has long been noted as it occurs following major separations (Darwin 1877; Robertson & Bowlby 1952) it has only recently (Ainsworth & Bell 1970; Ainsworth, Bell, & Stayton 1971) been observed that some young, home-reared children avoid the mother following even extremely brief experimental separations in a strange environment. Avoidance of the mother appearing in this context is relevant to a concern with social development and day-care, both because a significantly greater avoidance of the mother appears in day-care than in home-reared children separated and re-united in a strange environment (Blehar 1974 and in this volume) and because my own studies show an association between avoidance of the mother and social and affective disturbance.

I shall be suggesting in this chapter that avoidance indicates that the infant finds himself in a conflict situation. Data are presented indicating that in the case of nonseparated, home-reared children, avoidance of the mother is related not only to a pattern of disturbance in infant social and affective behavior but also to a specific pattern of maternal behavior.

The topic of this chapter is then the meaning—the history, function, and sequelae—of avoidance of the mother as it appears in a context in which approach to the mother would be instead expected.

AVOIDANCE

Avoidant behaviors are any behavior which serve to maintain or increase the distance between one individual and another specific individual: looking away, turning away, hiding the face, and moving away are examples of avoidant behavior. In addition, active failures to respond or interact when response or interaction is expected, i.e., active ignoring of specific individuals, can also be said to serve this purpose and in this sense can be classified as avoidant behavior.

The purpose of this initial section is simply to describe the behavior to be explained, avoidance, and the situations in which it commonly arises. My own studies of normal children focus upon avoidance of the mother as it appears in the "reunion" episodes of the Ainsworth Strange Situation, a brief laboratory test involving separation and reunion with the mother in the context of a strange environment (Ainsworth & Wittig 1969). The section, therefore, opens with a description of the strange situation, the theory of attachment which provided its conceptual base, and both the infant behavioral norm and two variants from that norm—one avoidant, and one not avoidant. We shall then consider avoidance as it appears in other contexts.

AVOIDANCE OF THE MOTHER IN THE STRANGE SITUATION

I. The Theory of Attachment

In order to begin to understand why it is interesting that some one-year-olds avoid their mothers following brief separations in a strange environment, it is necessary not only to understand that the behavior is uncommon, and therefore statistically unexpected but also that it is theoretically unexpected for infants of usual rearing. Since the strange situation test was devised in accordance with expectations derived from the theory of attachment developed by Bowlby (e.g., 1958, 1969, 1973) and by Ainsworth (1967, 1969, 1972), this section begins with a brief review of that "ethological-evolutionary theory." It is intended here only to show the conditions under which attachment behavior is expected, the conditions expected to lead to its diminution, and the reason why the attachment behavioral system is so readily activated (that is, the reason why maintaining proximity to the mother and, in times of heightened insecurity, achieving contact with her looms so high on the infant's list of behavioral priorities).

Attachment behaviors are behaviors which serve to maintain or increase proximity, contact, or interaction between individuals: crying, smiling, calling, clinging, and following are examples of attachment behaviors (Bowlby 1969). While a very young infant exhibits attachment behavior in such indiscriminate circumstances that no tie to a specific individual can be inferred, he normally develops over time a stable propensity to direct attachment behavior to one (or two, or three) specific individuals over others. As signs of his attachment, he then tends to cry when these but not other individuals leave him and to greet and to seek them actively when they return; to use these but not other individuals as a "secure base" from which to explore the animate and inanimate environment; and to fly to these but not other individuals as though to a haven of safety in times of alarm. The necessary conditions for the formation of this stable propensity or attachment are three (Ainsworth 1973): that the infant should be able to discriminate among figures; that he should have acquired the concept of object permanence sufficiently that "objects" are not entirely lost to him when they are not immediately present to his perceptions; and that he should have had sufficient social interaction (the exact amount is not yet specified) with the potential "attachment figure." Attachments to a "primary attachment figure"* are normally formed at about seven months of age, and it is extremely unlikely that a home-reared infant would fail to be attached to a primary attachment figure by twelve months, the time of the strange situation testing to be reported. Attachment behavior may thereafter be absent for a long period of time, yet (according to Ainsworth 1969) the attachment, tie, or bond itself remains as a stable propensity to seek the proximity of the attachment figure, a propensity assumed by Ainsworth to have some kind of intra-organismic, 'structural' basis. Put in another way, the presence, absence, and behavior of the attachment figure will continue to influence the young infants' behavior, once the infant is attached, whether or not the influence shows its effects in overtly exhibited attachment behavior.

According to Bowlby (1969), a review of literature describing the behavior of infants throughout the world and describing the behavior of nonhuman primates shows that attachment behavior is widespread, similar in form, and easily invoked over almost the entire primate species. This in turn suggests that a biological ("survival") function must be served by the behavior, since the potential for its development would not otherwise have been incorporated so broadly within the behavioral repertoire of the species. The "biological function" of a behavior is the function which gave the species survival advantage in the "environment of evolutionary adaptedness," the environment in which the behavior originally evolved. The original biological function of a behavior cannot be determined from a consideration of selection pressures

---

*Because the tie appears to be formed on the basis of social interaction rather than genes, a baby's primary attachment figure is only usually, and by no means necessarily, his biological mother.

operating in environments which do not closely approximate this original environment. Nor need the original biological function of a behavior be the functions it currently serves, or even the function which has served to maintain it within the repertoire. Nonetheless, the original biological function if successfully ascertained is, I believe, of interest for these important reasons: First, if we know one original biological function of a behavioral system, we have an explanation for the diverse conditions activating and terminating the activity of the system. This in turn gives clues to the likelihood that the system will be activated under certain conditions, whether or not the behavior is exhibited. Second, such knowledge gives clues to the immediacy or priority of the behavioral system. That is, to the likelihood that behaviors belonging to other specifiable systems of less immediate survival value will fail to be exhibited when the conditions for the activation of those systems are equally favorable.

Based on examination of the conditions "activating" and "terminating" the action of the "attachment behavioral system"; informed speculation regarding the nature of the "environment of evolutionary adaptedness"; and reasoning regarding the survival requirements of the relatively helpless human infant during the long years of human childhood, Bowlby has speculated that the initial biological function of attachment behavior was protection from predators. In the environment of evolutionary adaptedness, then, the young infant who did not keep in proximity to his adults was more vulnerable to predation and other dangers than other infants and would, in consequence, be less likely to leave progeny.

Bowlby believes this particular biological function accounts better than some alternatives (such as "Learning") for the conditions observed to activate attachment behavior in young infants. Conditions typically activating the behavior at low intensities (so that, for example, only a slow casual approach or a brief visual check is required) are slight changes in the environment, slight and slow increase in the distance between mother and child, and perhaps even (Bowlby 1969, citing unpublished data collected by Dorothy Heard) "elapsed" time since the last check was made on the whereabouts of the mother. Conditions typically activating the behavior at high intensities (so that rapid approach is perhaps combined with loud calling or crying) are conditions of the child leading to his increased vulnerability (ill health, fatigue, pain); the mother's absence, departure, or rebuff of proximity; and the occurrence of alarming events of diverse nature.

Conditions sufficient to terminate the child's display of attachment behaviors vary with the intensity of the original activation. As Bowlby states (1969), "when systems are intensely active nothing but physical contact with the mother herself will serve to terminate them. When systems are less intensely active sight of the mother or even sound of her may do." Conditions almost certainly requiring physical contact with the mother are strong pain, strong alarm, and strong maternal rebuff. If, as necessarily happens during major separations, the attachment behavioral system is continually and strongly activated without termination, anger results. Bowlby proposes this anger may initially serve the function of overcoming such obstacles as there may be to reunion, and even of discouraging the loved person from going away again. But, whatever its function, the anger that inevitably arises when the attachment behavioral system is strongly frustrated can easily become dysfunctional (Bowlby 1973).

Infant attachment is not well understood until its relation to exploration, play, and fear, is delineated, as well as the relation between the formation of early attachments and later social developments. As is true of other objects of inquiry,* the development and function of this infant behavioral system is of interest more for the sake of other behavioral systems it relates to and for the further development it portends than for itself alone.

The primate infant's attachment behavior, then, can be appreciated fully only when it is viewed as coupled with strong tendencies to move away from the mother to explore the animate and inanimate environment. One adaptive gain of a long period of infancy in which the infant is actively protected by the parent is that the infant may learn to adapt to the specific conditions of any one of a very diverse array of environments (Hamburg 1968). The proximity of the attachment figure provides a protected environment in which learning can take place, and exploratory behavior and attachment

---

*Including the unfortunate Anne Gregory described by W. B. Yeats.

behavior exist in a "dynamic balance." The infant normally explores the environment in the protection and perceived security of the mother's presence, moving close to her or otherwise checking on her whereabouts, then moving from her to explore, then moving closer again in smoothly alternating sequence. Observations of this smooth sequence have led some writers (Harlow 1961; Ainsworth 1967) to refer to the mother as providing a "secure base" for the infant's explorations. Relatedly, while the presence of the mother diminishes apparent fearfulness the absence of the mother strongly heightens it, a fact demonstrated not only in human but also in nonhuman studies (e.g., Sroufe et al., 1974; Bronson 1972).

Because the development of the attachment behavioral system depends upon experience, because later developments in any broadly conceived behavioral system depend to varying extent upon earlier developments, and because there is evidence (summarized in Bowlby 1969) for a "sensitive phase"* in the development of attachments, Bowlby hypothesizes that there is room for serious behavioral anomaly and deviance if the rearing conditions provided deviate strongly from those that existed in the environment of adaptedness. One extreme departure in rearing conditions is that the infant should have, throughout the entire sensitive phase for the formation of attachment, insufficient interaction with caretaking figures for the formation of a tie to any specific individual. In this case, as implied by the notion of the "sensitive phase", his ability to form ties to any specific individual thereafter, *may* become limited or fail altogether.† It should be emphaiszed once more, however, that almost all family-reared one-year-olds seen in the usual study settings (unless of course *for* reasons of abnormality) are attached to some primary figures. If they should then fail to exhibit attachment behavior under conditions in which it is expectable, we must look to some alternative explanations.

---

*"Sensitive phase" refers to a period of development during which the organism is especially vulnerable or responsive to the influences of environmental contingencies; alternately, a period in which learning of a particular type most readily takes place.

†This result still turns on his future experience of the environment. A sensitive phase differs critically from a critical period.

2. The Strange Situation

The strange situation is a brief (22-minute) situational test designed by Ainsworth and Wittig (1969) to illustrate the way in which exploratory behavior gradually gives way to attachment behavior when young children are subjected to minor stresses in an unfamiliar laboratory setting, and to highlight individual differences in the attachment relationship, as shown in differing infant responses. The eight episodes of the situation are so arranged that the less disturbing come first, and the situation is designed to be novel and interesting enough to elicit exploratory behavior in its opening episodes. The "stresses" to which the infants are subjected are, in order of their appearance, the entrance of a stranger into the room; a separation from the mother in which the infant is left in the company of a stranger; and a separation from the mother in which the infant is left alone.* The situation as a whole is intended to be no more disturbing than those an infant is likely to encounter in the course of ordinary life, and mothers are thoroughly familiarized with the procedures in advance. Since, as noted earlier, both Blehar's studies of differences between day-care and home-reared infants, and my own studies of two independent samples of home-reared infants center upon the strange situation, a detailed description of the procedures is provided here.

The strange situation is conducted in a laboratory room furnished with toys. A one-way mirror permits observation of child, mother, and stranger, and their behavior is recorded either by narrative dictation or by video camera. The eight episodes of the strange situation proceed in a standard order for all subjects, each, but the first, lasting three minutes unless curtailed in deference to infant distress.

One hundred and six one-year-old infants and their mothers have now been seen in strange situations conducted in Baltimore by Ainsworth, by Bell (1970), and by Main (1973). The white middle-class mothers and infants have been obtained with the cooperation of Baltimore pediatricians who have given us lists of normal babies

---

*For some rare (Group C) infants, even entering the strange environment in the company of the mother appears stressful.

from normal homes: surprisingly, only a very few mothers contacted have refused participation. Individual differences in response to the strange situation can be described in terms of the particular behaviors exhibited, including avoidant behaviors; in terms of the way in which infants are classified into strange situation groups, including a group of highly avoidant infants; and in terms of scores given for avoidance of the mother. We begin here with a description of particular behaviors. The description is taken from Ainsworth, Blehar, Waters, and Wall (1977).

For the great majority of babies, exploratory behavior gradually diminished over the eight episodes of the strange situation. In the second episode of the strange situation, before the entrance of the stranger into the room, almost all babies showed exploratory locomotion. By the first separation, only about one-third of the babies explored, and by the second separation, almost none. During the first separation, about half the babies cried, and during the second separation, over three-quarters. If babies were distressed by the mother's absence, it was difficult for the stranger to comfort them: babies picked up by the stranger often stiffened, squirmed, tried to get down, or increased the intensity of their crying. When the mother returned to the room during the reunion episodes, over three-quarters of the babies reacted to the mother by approaching, reaching, smiling, vocalizing, or crying. Approach was the most common reaction. When picked up by the mother, at her initiative or their own (within the first 15 seconds of episode eight a vast majority of the sample had achieved contact with the mother), about two-thirds of the infants clung to the mother or sank into her. A few kicked her or pushed her away.

About 12 percent of all babies seen in the strange situation fall in a heterogenous group, called Group C, loosely specified as showing "maladaptive" behavior. Many of these show distress even prior to separation, and most show extreme distress during separation, including heightened apparent fear, particularly shown with the stranger, and a general tendency to fear and distress. For this reason, perhaps, they explore very little or, if they do, explore in a disturbed manner. Reunited with the mother following separation, they both seek comfort strongly and are angrily resistant. In that fear, anger, and distress are so overtly exhibited, while exploration is diminished or disturbed they seem the mirror image of the avoidant, exploratory, "neutral" appearing babies, who are here our concern. While we will not further examine this type, it is important to recognize the existence of a type of baby other than the avoidant baby whose behavior and whose social relationships are also disturbed. *No claim is made here that all disturbances in infants and in infant-mother relations are of the type leading to avoidance of the mother and lack of affect display.* Indeed, were that the case, the story would be less interesting because less precisely told.

Let us now consider the avoidant behaviors shown by a substantial minority of the babies—often, the same babies whose exploration diminished little during and following separation, who cried little or none if left alone, and who were not unfriendly to the stranger. Avoidant behaviors are noted only during the reunion episodes. It is interesting to note that babies who avoid the mother during the reunion episode may well have approached or even touched her earlier. During the reunion episodes, however, the baby tends to treat the mother (and the mother treat the baby) in such a way that casual observers are likely to ask whether "that is not the baby and the stranger."

About one-fifth of the sample failed to greet the mother at reunion. A few individuals even failed to look at her. About the same number of infants as failed to greet the mother turned away from her after having looked at her or even after having greeted her, and four out of the 106 babies crawled or walked away. During the whole episode half of the sample showed at least a limited avoidance; some looked away, some turned away, and six even moved away. Twenty percent of the babies conspicuously ignored the mother at some point, failing to respond when addressed, or failing to acknowledge her by more than a momentary glance. Prolonged ignoring (lasting more than one minute) was infrequent, occurring in less than one-tenth of the infants. In the second reunion episode, a minority of babies were picked up by their mothers. About one-fifth of the babies held squirmed to get down, four leaned away, and three were totally unresponsive. A substantial minority of those held, then ignored or avoided or broke off from physical contact with the mother (Ainsworth, Blehar, Waters, & Wall 1977).

This lengthy description of the range of behaviors occurring in the strange situation (from Ainsworth et al. 1976) has been given because, as Medawar (1967) reminds us, "it is not informative to study variations of behavior unless we know beforehand the norm from which the variations depart." In studying avoidance throughout the remainder of this paper it will be helpful to recall that it is a variant from the norm that has earlier been described.

It is difficult to develop a system ordering babies in terms of avoidance exhibited. Not only are there many possible acts of visual avoidance, but there is also outright physical withdrawal and ignoring. Any and all of these acts may or may not be combined with active proximity seeking or signaling. In the case of ignoring, the mother's behavior as well as the baby's must be taken into account.

The Ainsworth scoring system for Proximity and Interaction Avoiding takes these multiple criteria into account. Points on her 7-point scale are defined by particular combinations of behaviors, and several examples are given for most points on the scale. The actual behaviors shown by the infant are therefore relatively well-defined and recoverable. The highest score on the scale is given to the baby who fails to greet his mother upon her return and who pays little or no attention to her for an extended period, despite the mother's efforts to attract his attention. Moderate scores are given to brief but clear-cut avoidance or persistent low-keyed avoidance, and a weak score is given to very brief delays in responding to the mother's return, or brief instances of mild avoidance.

Avoidance can be scored on the Ainsworth scale with high inter-scorer reliability, e.g., $r = .94$ for two raters working independently on 40 cases (Main 1973). It is also surprisingly stable: $r = .66$ when 23 infants were seen in successive strange situations separated by a two-week period (Ainsworth 1973).

Let us consider once more the cluster of behaviors typically shown by the superficially independent babies who avoid the mother during the reunion episodes of the strange situation. Babies who avoid the mother tend to show little attachment behavior in the form of approach or distress: if there is approach, it tends to be abortive; if picked up, they fail to respond, lean away, or squirm to get down; and if they cry on separation, it seems to be only because they are left alone. Affectively they seem neutral (or even cheerful), and just as little distress or attachment is shown, so little or no anger or fear is shown. The stranger is treated much as the mother is treated, a point that is emphasized by the fact that the behavior of the mother and the avoidant baby often leads casual observers to ask whether the woman currently in the room with the baby (in fact the mother) is not the stranger. (The stranger, however, may be treated by these babies with less, rather than more avoidance). Avoidant babies tend to explore at high levels throughout the strange situation.

Given the cluster of behaviors surrounding avoidance, as well as the subtlety of avoidance itself, it is perhaps not surprising that behavior of this type is taken as indicative of a desirable social independence or maturity—which is the interpretation usually given it, by maternal as well as casual professional observers.

Viewed in the light of the theory of attachment presented earlier, however, behavior of the type that appears in the mother-avoidant babies is more than passing strange. Events that should heighten attachment behavior serve only to diminish it, and behaviors exactly antithetical to attachment behavior appear in its place. Finally, the baby does not always merely appear neutral regarding physical contact; he often appears to actively dislike it, a strange appraisal of things for an infant of a species in which this "goal situation" (contact with the mother) is the ultimate signal of security in times of danger.

AVOIDANCE IN NORMAL INFANCY: SITUATIONALLY APPEARING AVOIDANCE

Visual avoidance appears in the earliest weeks of life. Robson (1967) observing babies who persistently avoided eye contact during the first three months of life, referred to a "predisposition to gaze aversion" and appealed to the potency of the "eye gestalt" as an evoker of gaze aversion or flight responses in animals as an explanation. Main and Brazelton in a microanalytic study of mother-infant communication sequences observed one infant repeatedly averting his gaze and even turning his head from his insistent mother—or at least, appearing to do so—in the neonatal period. Similarly, Stechler and Latz (1966) observed looking-away from a "stimulating" human face beginning at seventeen days. The infant they observed, like the infant observed by Main and Brazelton, gave the impression of deliberate avoidance. Somewhat later in infancy, Stern (1971) filmed twin boys in social play with their rather interfering mother several times over the first year of life, beginning at three and one-half months. One of these was consistently unable to hold a face-to-face position with other persons from three and one-half to fourteen months, and at twelve to fifteen months greeted people with a fearful expression, refusing to make prolonged eye contact. He regularly executed face aversions in social situations.

While visual avoidance at three months does not necessarily denote a well-defined affective response, its apparently deliberate quality ensures that it will affect a care-taker attempting to interact with the gaze-averting infant. On the part of the young baby, his avoidance is one of the few ways he has of dealing with unpleasant stimulation: he cannot get away from it and he cannot persuade it to leave him (Brazelton, Koslowski, & Main 1974).

According to Coss (1974) "normal children will show evidence of wary and shy behavior toward unfamiliar adults or angry parents. Gaze aversion, when it occurs under these conditions is often accompanied by turning the head and body away." Anger and fearfulness are frequently cited correlates of avoidance in older children. Goodenough (1932) observed a deaf-blind born girl turning her head as part of an expression of mild resentment, and Eibl-Eibesfeldt (1970) observed turning away of the head in a deaf-blind born girl as part of her response to strangers.

In the study of normal infants, avoidant behaviors as such are often of interest as they occur in confrontations between young infants and strangers. Bretherton and Ainsworth (1974) reported that 68/106 one-year-old infants averted their gaze from a stranger during the first three minutes of her entrance into their environment; and though mother and stranger were equally salient, none averted their gaze from the mother. In their analysis of gaze aversion and other acts of avoidance with respect to a stranger,

Bretherton and Ainsworth, like others (below), suggested that avoidant behaviors are indicative of a conflict between behavioral systems simultaneously activated by the stranger—a "fear wariness" system on the one hand, and an affiliative system on the other.

Bronson (1972) has studied infants' reactions to unfamiliar persons at three, four, six and one-half, and nine months. As the infants grew older, visual avoidance increased. By nine months the infants proved capable of limiting visual contact, even when the stranger picked them up, and some continued to ignore the stranger, displaying neutral affect, even when on the stranger's knee. Avoidance was, in fact, characteristically found associated with a neutral rating upon the affect rating scale developed by Bronson—but babies rated neutral and avoidant during a stranger's approach contrasted with those only rated neutral in that they were uneasy when picked up. Bronson saw visual avoidance as a valid indication of uneasiness and as occuring in situations in which affiliative orientation and wariness were simultaneously aroused. He speculated it might be a response unique to encounters with conspecifics, emerging phylogenetically as a "coping technique that did not preclude an eventual active social engagement." The latter speculation is similar to the Chance hypothesis, described below.

Like Bronson, Sroufe, Waters, and Matas (1974) found gaze aversion associated with "neutral" affect during stranger approaches. Later, Waters, Matas, and Sroufe (1975) uncovered a clear temporal relationship between heart rate acceleration and gaze aversion. Gaze aversion typically occurred just prior to the peak of a strong heart rate acceleration in infants who did not soon cry. The "wary avert gaze" of the baby confronted by the stranger could be described in some detail: "from either (wary brow) or (open expression) eyelids begin to close smoothly over the eyes as the face is turned down and away. This can be distinguished from simply looking elsewhere by the initial partial closing of the eyes, the absence of a blink or shift of the eyes to either side, and by the downward turn of the head." Like Bronson, these authors suggested gaze aversion is a developing mechanism for coping with stress, one which acts to modulate the infants' arousal (e.g., heart rate)* and

---

Editor's Note Heart rate changes are more parsimoniously interpreted as concomitants to movements of the subject. This does not mean, however, that heart

allow reengagement of the stranger. They suggest that gaze aversion may keep the infant from falling into an "all or nothing" response pattern, such as crying, which cannot be terminated voluntarily.

Like Bretherton and Ainsworth, Waters et al. looked for avoidance of the mother under the same conditions in which avoidance of the stranger had appeared (in this case, in the laboratory during a "mother approach") and failed to find it. There were no behavioral indices of wariness nor was there heart rate acceleration during mother approaches.

These studies, although dealing with avoidance of a stranger rather than a mother, parallel the avoidance discussed by Ainsworth and her colleagues and begin to instruct us regarding the nature of avoidance.

The physical movements of avoidance (such as turning away) and *ignoring* (as in failure to respond to being held) are placed by Bronson, as by Ainsworth, in the category of avoidance. The avoidant look away (Waters et al. "wary avert" gaze) can be distinguished from looking toward by careful study of video tape: this is instructive, since casual observers of the strange situation "see" the former as being identical to the latter and, therefore, like the latter indicative of real exploratory interest and independence. Finally and most importantly (1) the avoidance is again associated with a neutral facial expression—a neutrality belied by the heart rate data and by behavioral data; (2) it is hypothesized that the child is in conflict and that means of avoidance he retains control, or "modulates his arousal."

Avoidance in Response to Major Separation: "Detachment"

(Reggie's) second attachment was suddenly broken at 2 years 8 months when his "own" nurse married. He was completely lost and desperate after her departure, and refused to look at her when she visited him a fortnight later. He turned his head to the other side when she spoke to him, but stared at the door, which had closed behind her, after she had

---

rate is not a useful adjunct measure. See Webb, R. A., & Obrist, P. A., 1970. *Psychophysiology* 6: 389–403.

left the room. In the evening in bed he sat up and said: "My very own Mary-Ann! But I don't like her."

—Burlingham and Freud (1944)
quoted in Bowlby (1973) p. 4

As noted earlier, when the attachment behavioral system is activated for a long time without being terminated, i.e., without proximity or contact with the attachment figure being achieved, not only anxiety, but also anger, is the almost inevitable result (Bowlby 1973). One condition in which this situation necessarily arises is in major separations from the primary attachment figure. If the separation persists long enough, upon reunion the primary attachment figure is persistently avoided and is treated as a stranger. The child is then said to have entered the state of detachment.

Thus, when young children are separated from their attachment figures and placed in a strange environment with no substitute attachment figure made available to them, they at first exhibit heightened attachment behavior and, eventually, as is expectable given the strong frustration of the behavioral system, anger. During separation, anger is shown toward objects representing the parents and toward other objects, adults, and children apparently without provocation (e.g., Prugh et al. 1953; Heinecke & Westheimer 1965). During reunion there is a strongly increased tendency to temper tantrums (even in monkey children, see Spencer-Booth & Hinde 1966) and to *hostility* (e.g., hitting and biting the mother) and *negativism* (e.g., tantrums and refusals in which hostility is implied, although it is not so directly stated, Heinecke & Westheimer 1965). If the separation lasts longer, attachment behavior and angry behavior will gradually diminish; if the separation lasts long enough, upon reunion the primary attachment figure is persistently avoided.

When children are separated from their attachment figures for a long time under the conditions outlined above, they will most likely move into the three successive phases of response to separation first described by Robertson and Bowlby (1952): *protest, despair,* and (what is termed by them) *detachment.*

During the initial phase of *protest,* the child is acutely distressed at having lost his mother, and his attachment behavior is highly activated; he cries, calls, and searches for her if he is free to do so.

During the succeeding phase, *despair,* the child seems to be in deep mourning. The orientation to the mother's loss is unmistakable, but his behavior suggests hopelessness. His crying tends to be monotonous, muted, and intermittent. In each of these phases a visit from the mother tends to evoke both attachment behavior and anger—in short, ambivalence.

The child who has reached the phase of *detachment* tends to be described as "settled in" and back to normal (Ainsworth 1973). Bowlby (1969) describes the stage of detachment as follows:

> Because the child shows more interest in his surroundings the phase of detachment which sooner or later succeeds protest and despair is often welcomed as a sign of recovery. The child no longer rejects the nurses; he accepts their care and the food and toys they bring, and may even smile and be sociable. To some this change seems satisfactory. When his mother visits, however, it can be seen that all is not well, for there is a striking absence of the behavior characteristic of the strong attachment normal at this age. So far from greeting his mother he may seem hardly to know her; so far from clinging to her he may remain remote and apathetic; instead of tears there is a listless turning away. He seems to have lost all interest in her. (p. 28)

A more precise behavioral description is provided by Heinecke and Westheimer (1965) who studied ten two and three-year-old children undergoing separations from the parents lasting from three to twenty weeks. They observed the moment of reunion following separation and report:

> At the moment of reunion, all the separated children were unable to respond affectionately to the mother. In order of frequency this took the following forms: physical avoidance, remaining present but not responding with affection, and apparent lack of recognition. (p. 280)

> In two instances, doubt arose as to whether the child recognized his mother. For example, when Gillian was first confronted with her mother, she stared into space. . . .

> The other reaction, that of turning away or backing away, was observed in the remaining eight cases. The child either walked away from his mother or turned his face or back to her. . . . The reactions described were seen in relation to the mother and rarely in relation to the father. (pp. 215–16)

Turning away and/or refusing to look in response to reunion is also reported by Bowlby (1969) and Burlingham and Freud. Lack of recognition is also reported by Robertson (1953) and by Freud and Burlingham (1943). This lack of recognition is not indication of a general failure of memory: as Freud and Burlingham point out, and as I am personally aware from reports made to me by mothers, the father and the furniture are remembered where the mother seems forgotten. "She didn't know me, but she knew her father."

As noted earlier, the initial response to reunion described above need not last long: in most cases, it is soon replaced by an ardent, excessive, readily aroused attachment behavior ("anxious attachment," Bowlby 1973) and by hostility and negativism (Heinecke & Westheimer 1965). In some cases, however (particularly where the separation has been very long, or where many separations have occurred) the avoidance and apparent lack of recognition become consolidated, so that not only former attachment figures but also potential attachment figures are treated as the mother is treated —that is, in the case of the detached child, like strangers. In his book, *Attachment* (1969), Bowlby further describes the stage of detachment:

> Should his stay in hospital or residential nursery be prolonged and should he, as is usual, have the experience of becoming transiently attached to a series of nurses each of whom leaves and so repeats for him the experience of the original loss of his mother, he will in time act as if neither mothering nor contact with humans had much significance for him. . . . He will become increasingly self-centered and, instead of directing his desires and feelings toward people, will become preoccupied with material things such as sweets, toys, and food. . . . He will cease to show feelings when his parents come and go on visiting day; and it may cause them pain when they realize that, although he has an avid interest in the presents they bring, he has little interest in them as special people. He will appear cheerful and adapted to his unusual situation and apparently easy and unafraid of anyone. But this sociability is superficial: he appears no longer to care for anyone. (p. 28)

These peculiar avoidant behaviors directed away from the attachment figure or those associated with that figure in the mind of the child can, according to Heinecke and Westheimer (and others, cf.

Bowlby 1960; Ainsworth & Bell 1970) best be understood as serving a defensive function, permitting the child to maintain control over his anger (and probably too his distress). Although without precise behavioral descriptions supplemented by the kind of verbal self-report one-year-olds are unlikely to make we cannot really be sure what behavioral system is aroused, it is striking to note the parallel in interpretation: avoidance of strangers permits the child to maintain control over fear (Walters et al. 1975); avoidance of the mother permits him to control his anger.

Children who have reached the stage of detachment following major separations and mother-avoidant babies in the strange situation test act much alike, as indeed Ainsworth (Ainsworth & Bell 1970) has already noted. Like the avoidant babies, the detached children ignore the comings and goings of their mothers; like them they often do not cry; like them they do not cling; and like them, of course, they turn away. Like many avoidant children, the detached children seem neutral, or even cheerful, and certainly unafraid. They do not reject strange people and may even be sociable with them, as may the avoidant babies. Again, like the avoidant babies they seem preoccupied with material things such as toys. For all of these reasons they are considered by those who casually observe them, again in parallel, to be doing well.

There are, of course, a number of factors affecting the degree of disturbance which may follow a separation, and these are listed by Ainsworth (1973). Among these are the quality of the previous mother-child relation (children who have experienced a good relationship with the mother seem to slip less readily than others into detachment) and, the maturity of the child at the time of separation. Robertson and Bowlby (1952) found that children under three years of age were more likely than older children to pass from anxiety states during major separations into detachment. Another suggestion that maturity is an important variable is found in the only experimental study of nonhuman primates in which substantial mother-avoiding behavior was found following separation. In this study (by Abrams, cited in Bowlby 1973) distinguished from other monkey separation studies by the young age of the subjects, the infants ran away from the mother as she approached them upon reunion. Finally, in Blehar's study (1974 and in this volume) comparing day-care with home-reared children in the strange situation test, it was found that the greatest avoidance of the mother occurred in the younger day-care children.

Let us now consider one more description of behavior. In their study of responses to hospitalization in human infants, Schaeffer and Callendar (1959) reported differences in response according to whether the infants were above or below the age of twenty-eight weeks, the age at which they suggested (on the basis of the data presented in this study) specific attachments are first formed.

Infants above the age of twenty-eight weeks responded to hospitalization with protest, and many of them rejected strange persons. Infants below twenty-eight weeks did not reject strange persons but rather maintained their normal responsiveness; in the hospital their most striking quality was their unwonted silence. When returned to their homes, these younger children for minutes, hours, or days exhibited a syndrome which Schaeffer and Callendar entitled *Extreme preoccupation with the environment:*

> When the 28 infants of this group were returned home, they were, according to the reports of the mothers, "strange" in their behavior and the main feature of this "strangeness" consisted in excessive attention to the environment. For hours on end an infant might crane his neck, scanning his surroundings as though completely absorbed by them, yet without focusing on any particular feature. This preoccupation was so intense that it was usually impossible to distract the child with toys or elicit any form of normal responsiveness to people, and many of the mothers became quite disturbed by their failure to make contact with the babies during this time. The infants were subdued and quiet, usually staring around with the blank expressions though one or two were reported to have cried or whimpered.

Some of the children above twenty-eight weeks also initially showed "environmental preoccupation" upon reunion, but this was succeeded by "overdependence"—the name these workers give to the syndrome of heightened attachment behavior and heightened anxiety which Bowlby describes as "anxious attachment."

Even if this behavior cannot be called detachment, on the grounds that only an attached child can show detachment, still it is interesting in that it is so strongly analogous to the behavior of both detached and avoidant children described earlier. The baby does not cry; he has a blank expression; people cannot make contact with him; and he shows unusual attention to the environment.

SPECULATIONS CONCERNING ETIOLOGY

1. Conflict and "Cut-off"

Many investigators of avoidance have, directly or indirectly, interpreted avoidance as conflict behavior. Each of the investigators of infant response to strangers cited earlier attributed avoidance to a conflict between a "fear-wariness" system on the one hand and an affiliative system on the other. Those observing children's response to major separation have also attributed avoidance to a conflict, one in which anger is aroused. In his Nobel prize acceptance speech, the ethologist Niko Tinbergen (1974) has recently also ascribed the avoidant behaviors of autistic children to conflict, noting (as we have here) that normal children often show autistic behavior, that is, "passing attacks of autistic behavior appear in a normal child when it finds itself in a situation that creates a conflict between two incompatable motivations." He reasons that naturally timid children are, more than others, likely to find themselves in an approach/avoidance conflict.

Thus, there appears to be an agreement between an ethologist, clinicians, and developmental psychologists that avoidance, in human infants, indicates conflict. If this is true in the strange situation as elsewhere, other aspects of the behavior of mother-avoiding babies become less puzzling.

If babies avoiding the mother in the strange situation are evidencing a confict between major behavioral systems as proposed by Main (1973), rather than indicating independence and a lack of interest, then other aspects of their behavior are perhaps also made more understandable. Their failure to exhibit attachment behavior in this situation, which to most psychologists apparently "operationally" proves them unattached, may be attributed to inhibition of the system rather than its failure ever to have developed—an attribution which better fits with Ainsworth's observation that by the end of the first year of life, by home observation, virtually every family-reared baby is attached.

Exploration of the room and its objects, continuing through episodes of separation and reunion, might be best termed a displacement activity, or more accurately, an activity "disinhibited" by the simultaneous activation of competing behavioral systems. Exploration, like grooming, is a frequently observed outcome of conflict in nonhuman animals (see Hinde 1966).

While attributing avoidant behaviors to "conflict" is helpful, in that it argues against an overly simplistic interpretation, we still need to know why conflict has the effect of producing avoidance, and why these behaviors appear when they do. To begin to answer these questions, we shall consider the work of Michael Chance.

In 1962 Michael Chance introduced the term "cut-off" to describe a type of behavior seen in rats, terns, and other birds in the context of an approach/avoidance conflict. Chance's hypothesis regarding the function of this behavior for the performing animal is well summarized in the abstract that begins his paper:

> Animals threatened by a member of their own species, for which they show at the same time evidence of attraction, adopt postures which effectively cut off the aggressive partner from view. These are called "cut-off" acts and postures. The examples discussed are social encounters between rats, the courtship of the Black-headed Gull, preening in nesting terns, and some aspects of the reproduction behavior of the Booby. From these examples it can be deduced that the "cut-off" postures may enable the threatened animal to remain close to its partner.

> This is because the sight of the partner may be expected to raise the aversive drives of flight and aggression at the start of a social encounter and perhaps at all times during social behavior (e.g., during courtship). Owing to the arousal value of the stimulus provided by the parnter, removing the partner from sight could be expected to facilitate the lowering of these drives in a threatened animal.

The movements that Chance is describing are any movements which have the effect of cutting off a conspecific; turning away the eyes, turning the head away or down, displacing or redirecting the attention, and closing the eyes are thus examples of "cut-off" acts and postures.

It is obvious that Chance assumes that the sight of conspecifics, for whatever reason of history or predisposition, "arouses" an animal, and does so usually in more than one way—and often in several, as in courtship when tendencies to flee and to attack combine with sexual tendencies. The sequence of postures in-terspersed with cut-off postures adopted by the Black-headed Gull during courtship in fact strongly suggest to Chance that first flight, then attack tendencies are modulated by the cut-off postures.*

While Chance recognizes the elements of flight within cut-off, he emphasizes that it is the maintenance of proximity that is the outcome: "Rats often merely turn their head away from another threatening rat. Be this as it may be an intention movement of flight, it may also enable the arousal produced by the threat to wane and hence enable the rat to stay where it is."

Chance emphasizes other gains to cut-off also. Cut-off permits the performing animal to gain control over, i.e., flexibility in his own behavior, a thing which he will not have should he actually flee (or in the case of young babies, break into disorganized distress). The animal is "freed from an increasing compulsive limitation of its behavior into one channel." If this immediate gain is accurate, then brief avoidance in conflict situations producing high arousal seems in some circumstances an adaptive, even admirable way of dealing with distress.

The Chance hypothesis that visual avoidance functions to reduce arousal has been accepted by several investigators of infant response to strangers (see Sroufe et al. 1974; & Waters et al. 1975) and indeed the heartbeat data presented in the latter study alone (cited earlier) would tend to corroborate it. In this later case, again, it is a fear-wariness system that is presumed modulated by the infant's gaze aversion.

The more startling aspects of the Chance hypothesis, however, when we consider the overtly avoidant nature of avoidant move-

---

*In other words (to simplify greatly) a posture normally suggesting that the bird is about to take flight is succeeded by cut-off, and this by the posture thought most likely to go over to attack (in the Black-head Gull, the "upright posture") which is again succeeded by cut-off. The service performed by cut-off is that the animals hold their ground. The female neither attacks nor flees, and the male, doing likewise, eventually works his wicked way with her.

ments, are surely these two: that it is supposed that the avoidant movement may serve to modulate *any* tendencies at all; and that it is supposed that the proper explanation of the avoidant movement, even when it is flight that is being modulated, is not merely that the performing animal is fleeing from the second animal a little bit, but that the movement is useful to him because it enables him to do so *only* a little bit—in short, that through avoidance he maintains proximity.

It remains to be seen whether avoidance of the mother in the strange situation can also readily be interpreted as cut-off: here too, studies of heart rate (conducted by E. Waters, and to date affirmative) are under way. It should be remembered, however, that cut-off refers to conflict, a conflict engendered, in Chance's words, by an aggressive or threatening social partner—and that at any rate conflict regarding the appearence of the mother is hardly to be expected.

2. Conditions Leading to Avoidance of the Mother in the Strange Situation: Hypotheses

> *Perhaps this singular piece of apparent stupidity may be accounted for by the circumstance, that this reptile has no enemy whatever on shore, whereas at sea it must often fall prey to the numerous sharks. Hence, probably, urged by a fixed and hereditary instinct that the shore is its place of safety, whatever the emergency may be, it there takes refuge.*

Darwin, *Voyage of the Beagle,* 1972

If avoidance of the mother in the strange situation is indeed an example of cut off behavior, and "cut-off" is indicative of a conflict occurring between attachment behavior and some other form of behavior, we need now to ask, conflict with what other major behavioral system and due to what kind of previous experience?

Following major separations it has been supposed anger has eventually arisen and is modulated (or defended against) through visual cut-off (through avoidance). But in the strange situation we deal with children who have not been separated from the mother for any major period—not in the previous year, and certainly not in the strange situation. The question then is, through what specific process, through what specific events, might these children come to behave like children who *have* suffered major separations? We seem to have here something very like detachment arising, strangely, in attached children living continually in the company of their mother in the home situation.

I would like to suggest that three principles or observations (each one found in Bowlby 1969 or 1973) are sufficient to permit us to infer a process through which a family-reared infant might come to avoid his mother. These are (1) that alarm from any source leads to intense activation of the attachment behavioral systems, (2) that when these systems are intensely active only physical contact with the mother herself will serve to terminate them, and (3) that when for a long time the attachment behavioral systems are activated without reaching termination, anger is the almost inevitable outcome. The complexities and contingencies here involved deserve some elaboration.

I. As we normally conceive of the workings and functions of the attachment behavioral system, the child who is alramed—by thunder, by threats from other adults, or by "predators"—inevitably seeks his mother, who is in times of fear his single haven of security or safety. But if alarm from *any* source leads to strong activation of the systems, then the systems must be highly activated, even when the mother herself is the source of alarm, the child will seek her though she is herself his predator.

As Bowlby states, then (1969) for the young infant, maternal rebuff (or any maternal behavior which threatens the child's proximity) leads to particularly intense and active proximity-seeking. That the system works in this way has been corroborated in several studies of monkey behavior: monkeys return relentlessly to their mothers despite rejection (Kaufman & Rosenblum 1969) and even show stronger preference for their rejecting mothers than do infants of other normal monkey mothers (Sackett et al. 1967). That this is true for human children as well is a matter of simple fact to those attempting to remove young children from the homes of their abusing parents.

Though novelists (e.g., Hardy, Dostoevski, Maugham) and others have long been aware of the attraction irrationally implicit in rejection even in adulthood, the inevitable interworkings of the responsible infant behavioral systems have perhaps not been so plainly understood prior to the development of the attachment theory. An identical phenomenon with an almost identical explanation was, however, noted over one hundred years ago by Charles Darwin, as he stood on the shores of the Galapagos abusing a sea-lizard and tossing it into the sea. Although possessed of perfect powers to swim away from him, the reptile refused to leave the shore, and when thrown into the sea each time swam back to the point on which he stood. His explanation of "this singular piece of apparent stupidity" is given in the inset to this section: if the source of the attack is "the shore" itself, the shore is nonetheless returned to as a haven of safety.

We can hardly suppose, however, that such an attack—from a mother or from a Darwin—elicits only one response, that of a trusting approach to the attacker. Any "attack," even from an attachment figure, must elicit some fear. From this *single signal* then (one that is likely to be nonverbal, as when a mother shouts at her child or strikes him) at least *two* conflicting messages are received: to go from, and to come toward, the attachment figure.

It should be understood that this double and conflicting response to another person's threatening behavior is a phenomenon most likely to occur with reference to primary attachment figures, and perhaps it is most likely early in childhood. In adulthood the abusive shouts of bus drivers, sales clerks, and other passers-by merely repel us and do not drive us to them. It may also be the case that, "threats" of a given intensity coming even from primary attachment figures do not so greatly "attract" normal adults as young children, the system being less readily activated in older persons, and there being at the same time a greater number of alternate attachment figures for them than for many young children.

It should be understood that although theoretically any "threat" from the mother should momentarily activate competing tendencies, if the mother in fact then permits the child to approach her the competition or conflict should not be longlasting. This is the usual case. It is exemplified when the mother loudly and suddenly prohibits exploratory behavior of some type, but does not then prohibit the child from coming to her for contact and for comfort. Little conflict and certainly little ambivalence regarding the mother develops in this circumstance. The system frustrated is the exploratory, not the attachment system, and the possibility for approach succeeds so quickly the inherently conflicting signal that the momentary approach/withdrawal conflict is immediately resolved.

II. According to Bowlby (1969) maternal rebuff activates the attachment systems intensely, and when they are intensely activated only physical contact will serve to terminate them.

In our consideration of conflict it is important then to know that a few mothers actively discourage physical contact between themselves and their infants, either (usually) because they find physical contact with the young baby distasteful or because, while not having a special dislike for contact, they nonetheless have provided the baby with highly unpleasant experiences of it. If such a mother also actively rebuffs her infant so that he must approach her for physical contact, but does not allow him to establish physical contact, the resultant approach/withdrawal conflict is irresolvable. The conflict is now serious, deep, and nonverbal. A single movement on the part of the mother, intended to drive the child from her, at least initially brings him anxiously towards her—yet he cannot contact her, though only contact would terminate the activity of the system. The importance of physical contact to the attachment behavioral system will be elaborated in a paper that is in preparation (Main & Ainsworth 1977).

III. When the attachment behavioral system is continually activated without termination, anger is the almost inevitable result (Bowlby 1973). In the situation described above, the infant is in a state of continual activation without termination (that is, of frustration) with respect to his primary attachment figure. Like the infant long separated from the mother in a strange environment with no substitute care-taker available to him, this infant, who cannot obtain physical contact with his mother when only physical contact with her will satisfy him, is placed in a situation in which strong anger must develop. Conflicting with attachment, this anger may lead to situationally appearing visual cut-off even in early infancy. As the pattern of interaction continues over time, that is, as the conflict between attachment and withdrawal persists, and as aggression attendant upon unrelieved frustration develops and enters into the conflict, a stronger avoidance of the mother may appear and become increasingly consolidated. Aggression toward a primary attachment figure, perhaps particularly toward one that is already rejecting, can hardly be expressed without increasing the mother-infant distance that is already the child's problem. Anger, attachment, and withdrawal could then all be aroused by situations which for some children engender only attachment behavior. It would not be surprising if we found avoidance of the mother in these children, following brief separation in a strange environment.

3. Conditions Associated with Avoidance of the Mother in the Strange Situation: Data

Stated most simply, I have on theoretical grounds, hypothesized that home-reared children may come to avoid the mother in the strange situation because conflicting tendencies are activated, and that these will arise if they have repeatedly been rebuffed by the mother, especially if to the mother's more general anger, rebuff, or rejection is added experience which discourages the child from physical contact.

Certainly more distinct "predictions" might be made, but they have yet to be systematically examined (and, indeed, their examination would call for larger samples than those described below). If a mother is irritable but likes and never rebuffs physical contact and is otherwise affectionate, communicative, and calm, the baby should not be avoidant as babies of mothers in whom angry behavior and a rebuffing of contact combine. If, however, anger and a rebuff of contact do combine, the child would be more likely to become avoidant the younger he is at the time; moreover, he should suffer greater degrees of social and affective disturbances if he has no alternate attachment figures, so that no haven of security is provided him.

SAMPLES AND METHODS

The data summarized here are drawn from two independent samples of white middle-class Baltimore mothers and their babies. All babies were obtained through the assistance of Baltimore

pediatricians, and almost all mothers contacted agreed to to participate in the studies. The babies were normal, the sexes fairly equally
represented.

All babies were seen in the strange situation at one year of age.
For every baby scores for avoidance of the mother were assigned in
accordance with the Ainsworth scale. As noted earlier, about 20
percent of normal babies are highly avoidant, but about 50 percent
show at least slight avoidance.

The first, *Ainsworth* samples of babies and mothers were seen
roughly every three weeks over the first year of life, from three to
fifty-four weeks of age. Each visit lasted approximately four hours.
Home observers took extremely detailed notes on the ongoing
mother-infant interaction and dictated them following the visit: the
transcribed narrative record of a single visit is generally over twenty
single-spaced pages. Twenty-three of the twenty-six babies originally observed in this sample were also observed in the strange
situation testing. It is only these twenty-three babies who concern us
here. Reference to the "avoidant" Ainsworth babies made hereafter
is reference to the six babies classified in Group A. References to
avoidance are references to all infant scores for avoidance.

The second, *Main* sample of thirty-eight babies and mothers
was collected by myself for my (1973) doctoral thesis. This study
began with the strange situation at twelve months. The babies were
next seen in toddlerhood when at 20.5 months they came into the
laboratory for a Bayley testing session. At twenty-one months they
returned again to the laboratory for an hour-long video taped play
session. This play session took place in a large pleasant room
decorated like a living room, containing a shag rug, a blue velvet
sofa, flowers, bright posters, a mobile, and many toys.

The mother was present with the toddler throughout the play
session. For all but the last ten minutes of the session (mother-child
play) she was instructed to respond to the child as necessary, but not
to direct his activities. The hour-long session involved the following:
ten minutes of child play (the child was simply left to explore or play
as he chose in his mother's presence); twenty minutes of playmate
play (a woman with whom the baby was slightly familiar entered the
room to invite him to play a series of games with her); twenty
minutes of child play (as above); and a final ten minutes of mother-
child play (the mother was instructed to play with the toddler in any

way she found comfortable or natural). All assistants working on the Main play session data have been blind regarding strange situation behavior.

Two honors theses have now been completed, each using the data collected in the above study. Tomasini (1975) has assessed several aspects of maternal behavior during the play session, basing her work in part on narrative descriptions she has made from the video tapes, in part working directly from the tapes themselves. Tolan (1975) has taken slides of maternal facial expressions during the beginning minutes of playmate play. Tomasini, Tolan, and their assistants have all worked without knowledge of the infant's strange situation behavior earlier observed in the Main study. The procedures used in the Main, Tomasini, and Tolan studies will be described further as necessary.

ANGER, REBUFF, AND REJECTION

The difficult task of devising a coding system for those aspects of maternal anger or rebuff important to the infant is as yet only in the planning stages for both the Ainsworth and the Main samples. The required coding will be extremely difficult, since it is likely that not only specific events but also ongoing facial expressions and even body postures must be taken into account in order to fully assess the extent to which "rebuff" might be communicated to the child. For both samples, preliminary ratings have been undertaken however; in both samples, ratings of rejection have been made and in the Main sample, an effort to specifically assess the mother's anger through rating has also been made. All relationships reported here are significant unless otherwise noted.

Ainsworth and her colleagues (Ainsworth, Bell, & Stayton, 1971) rated each mother in the Ainsworth sample for her acceptance vs. rejection of her child as shown during the last quarter of the first year of life. While this was based upon other behavior where possible, ratings were largely based upon what the mother said about or to the child. It was necessarily taken as a sign of rejection if, for example, the mother said that she wished she had never had this child. (We must therefore conclude that these ratings for rejection are based more upon behaviors correlated with, than upon behaviors identical to, the means through which the mother's anger and rebuff could be communicated to the not-yet-one-year-old-child.) Working with the Main sample, Tomasini and her assistants used an adaption of the Ainsworth scale for acceptance vs. rejection to rate mothers for their rejection of their toddlers as shown during the ten minutes of mother-child play. This rating was based upon direct but repeated viewings of the video tape.

Still further repeated viewings of the tapes permitted Tomasini to develop highly detailed narrative records of maternal expressions of *anger* during both mother-child play and the first ten minutes of child play within the play session. Mothers were then rated on a seven-point scale for anger toward the child: anger rating was made by an assistant* who worked without knowledge of the ratings given for rejection. Surprisingly, in view of the brevity of the session and the mothers' awareness of the fact of the video taping, many expressions of anger were seen within these twenty minutes. Some expressions were direct and readily understandable, as they occurred when the child was disobedient or destructive, but some, though still direct, seemed oddly inappropriate—one mother, of an avoidant infant, was unquestionably irritated with her child for "spilling" an imaginary cup of tea. While some mothers simply scolded their infants in angry tones, some mocked them, spoke sarcastically to or about them, or stared them down. In some mothers whose faces and voices otherwise gave the impression of an almost eerie sweetness and/or self-control,† only fleeting expressions of disgust or anger could be seen; these mothers seemed to have the intent of not showing anger at all.

The correlation between the mother's rejection of her infant between nine and twelve months in the A sample and the infant's avoidance of his mother at twelve months was high,** as was the

---

*Phyllis Levin

†Careful review of the tape convinced Tomasini and myself that an anger carefully held in check was at least partially responsible for oddities (odd stress, slow tones, a hypnotic quality) of voice in one mother of an avoidant baby: the eventual coding of angry behavior will clearly not be a simple matter.

**Ainsworth, Bell, and Stayton (1971) as noted earlier did the original ratings, but presented the data somewhat differently than it is presented here. They showed in their paper that mothers of the highly avoidant Group A infants received the lowest

correlation between avoidance and the mother's anger with the infant at twenty-one months in the Main sample. Maternal rejection in the ten minutes of mother-child play at twenty-one months was also related to avoidance.

THE PHYSICAL CONTACT RELATIONSHIP

The Ainsworth sample (Main & Ainsworth 1976) has been studied in detail for evidence bearing upon the infant's experience in physical contact with his mother. The following aspects of maternal behavior are being taken into account: the mother's manner of holding the infant; the mother's manner of responding to the infant when he attempts to initiate contact with her; and the mother's expressed attitude to physical contact (with the infant, or with people in general, so long as the infant is obviously included in the latter category).

In the Ainsworth sample, our findings to date show that some mothers of babies who later come to avoid them have complained that they do not like physical contact; some have tended to hold the babies awkwardly or rigidly if at all, and may arch away from the baby if he becomes too intimate with them while held; some at sometime actively rejected the baby's initiations of contact. One mother pulled back and said angrily, "Stop it!"; another turned her face away immediately upon the initiation; another yelled, "Don't touch me!"; and another shoved the baby's head down into the crib until he stopped trying to get up.

The dislike for physical contact shown by most mothers of highly avoidant babies have been obvious. In one case, however, little dislike of contact was observed on the part of the mother, but the baby's experiences in contact were disturbing. In feeding him, his mother held the child on her lap in an uncomfortable posture, strapping his arms down, pinching his cheeks open, and forcing food in. At other times (outside the feeding situation) she simply

---

ratings for acceptance vs. rejection of any mothers in the Ainsworth sample. In my doctoral thesis (Main 1973) I simply correlated the latter ratings with the actual scores assigned for avoidance ($r=.69$, $N=23$) as reported above.

forced the baby, physically, to adopt postures she wished of him. Even in the home situation this baby came to combine his approaches with suddenly veering away from his mother.

To date in the analysis of the Ainsworth sample, it seems that whenever a mother and baby have had this kind of a strongly negative physical contact relationship, the baby has come to avoid the mother in the strange situation. But the converse does not completely hold. One or two babies who avoid the mother in the strange situation seem to have had such negative experiences to a lesser degree than the others who have avoided. Analyses of the data now being undertaken indicate that these babies have had some experience of separation (the mother may have left for a week's vacation) not long previous to the strange situation. This experience, in combination with some previous difficulty in the mother-infant relation, may have been sufficient frustration to the attachment systems to lead to avoidance in the strange situation.

Working with the Main sample, Tomasini (1975) wrote extensive narrative descriptions of all maternal behavior witnessed during the first ten minutes of child play, and the ten minutes of mother-child play, that could in any way indicate a negative attitude to physical contact on the part of the mother (or that could indicate that the toddler might have had negative experiences in contact). Mothers were then rated on a seven-point scale which took four aspects of the mother's (necessarily nonverbal) behavior into account: actual instances of shrinking back from the toddler as he approached, or adopting an odd or uncomfortable posture, the relaxation of which would bring the mother and toddler into physical contact; the mother's rough handling of the baby (most often seen in moving him from one place to another); rigidity of the mother's posture; and the distance the mother kept from the toddler. These are given in the same order in which they were given importance in the scale: mothers would be given quite high scores if they only shrank back from their children, or moved them about "none too gently," but they were given only very low scores if they only remained physically distant.

The video tapes of the play session clearly cannot provide the kind of data that is provided in the Ainsworth narrative records. The mothers say nothing on the tapes about their general attitude to contact, nor is it conceivable that a mother in that session would shout "Don't touch me!" to her approaching toddler. There is, nonetheless, a significant relation between the mother's negative attitude to physical contact and her infant's avoidance of her nine months previously.

OTHER MATERNAL CHARACTERISTICS: RIGIDITY AND LACK OF FACIAL EXPRESSION

The work above was undertaken in the interests of determining whether the hypothesized relation between avoidance, anger, and contact existed. In the course of studying the data, and without particular expectations or hypotheses, two additional characteristics of the mothers of avoidant babies come to light. The first appears in the Ainsworth data and has yet to be completely substantiated: that is, that the mothers of avoidant babies more than the mothers of other babies tend to be compulsive, mechanical, orderly, and rigid. The second characteristic, a general lack of expressiveness, especially of facial expression, also appears in the Ainsworth data. Work with the Ainsworth narrative data concerning this lack of expressiveness is not yet finished. Both Tomasini and Tolan, however, have devoted a portion of their honors theses to assessments of maternal expressiveness from my video taped records of mother-infant interaction at twenty-one months.

As part of the work undertaken in his (1975) honors thesis, Tolan took slides of (video tapes of) maternal facial expression during that portion of playmate play when toddler and playmate were engaged in a game of ball. Slides were taken at this time, both because the mothers could correctly assume that our then focus of interest was upon their child and the playmate, and because their activity (playing to happy music) was the activity in the play session which we thought most likely to evoke expression in most mothers. The slides were masked so that only the mother's face could be seen. They were rated for expressiveness by an assistant who had never seen the tapes. Tolan and I have found a strong negative relation between the mean score given mothers for facial expressiveness during the game of ball and avoidance of the mother by her infant nine months previously.

Tomasini (1975) in writing her extensive narrative description of maternal behavior during the first ten minutes of child play and during mother-child play paid special attention to *general* (facial, vocal, body) maternal lack of expressiveness. An assistant* then rated the mothers for their lack of facial expression. High scores were given to mothers who showed no facial expression, even where expression of pleasure (for example, when the child turned to the mother to share some object he was pleased with) or displeasure (when, for example, the child deliberately struck the mother or even threw something at her), would have been highly appropriate. Lower scores were given to mothers whose expressiveness was only occasionally limited.

Neither Tomasini nor Tolan had seen the portions of the video tape dealt with by the other. Despite the strong differences in the nature of the data collected by them, Tomasini's general *lack* of expressiveness (based on twenty minutes of observation) and Tolan's facial expressiveness (based on approximately five slides per mother) are significantly correlated.

More important, however, is the fact that Tomasini's general lack of expressiveness is substantially correlated with avoidance of the mother at nine months previous.

The mother's lack of facial expression may occur in direct reaction to having an avoidant baby (babies who strongly avoid the mother also act "odd" in other ways, and are unusually aggressive, as will be shown below). In this case her lack of expression need not relate to her own characteristics but only the baby's, and it need play no causal role in his unusual behavior.†

It is, on the other hand, possible that we see here a "syndrome." The mothers of avoidant babies who seem angry seem to us also to attempt to mask their anger more than other mothers. The anger, the dislike of physical contact, the masking of the anger, and the general lack of affect may constitute a kind of syndrome in which even the rigidity noted in the Ainsworth data may constitute a behavioral component.

---

*Phyllis Levin.

†Tomasini reports moderately high (.5–.6) intercorrelations between anger, a negative attitude to contact, and lack of facial expression (1975). These correlations are of the same strength as the relation between lack of expression and the baby's avoidance of the mother.

Of the behaviors constituting this syndrome, it could be that only the mother's directly expressed anger and her rebuffing of the infant's efforts at physical approach and contact have direct connection with the infant's avoidant behavior. The mother may be inexpressive because of her anger, but her inexpressiveness may not affect her baby. It seems more likely, however, that the lack of expression in the mother's face constitutes still another kind of "rebuff" from the viewpoint of the baby. A mother and infant become attached to one another, and express their mutual concern, not only by proximity seeking and physical contact but also by mutual gazing (Robson 1967) and by "play" which includes a "play" of facial expressions (see Stern 1973; Main & Brazelton 1975; cf. also Watson 1970). If the mother, no matter what the baby does, fails to react to him and maintains her same expression, the baby may well be frustrated and avoid her—just as the babies in the studies cited earlier (Brackbill 1958) avoided an experimentally impassive face.

As mentioned earlier, researchers other than Ainsworth and her colleagues have focused not upon avoidance of the mother, but upon various "discrete attachment behaviors" as measures of infant strange situations behavior. The correlations between five different discrete behaviors (crying, touching, smiling, looking, vocalizing) and the theoretically important maternal behaviors considered here have also been computed, working with the Main play session data. These correlations are, as they should probably be expected to be, insignificant.

CORRELATES OF AVOIDANCE

From knowing that avoidance appears in conflict situations; from knowing the social and affective disturbances shown by children who have reached the detachment phase of response to major separations; and from having discovered the association between avoidance of the mother and the particular group of maternal behaviors described above we should expect to find at least some social and affective disturbance on the part of the avoidant babies when observed outside of the strange situation. Examination of the Ainsworth and Main data have at least yet to disconfirm this expectation. Avoidance of the mother is associated with angry behavior; with an unwillingness or inability to interact even with persons other than the mother; with difficulties in the infant's physical contact relationship; and with a number of odd behaviors including stereotypes in some babies.

The babies are, then, as will be delineated below, difficult. This fact, and questions no doubt raised by the sequence of observations in my own study (*Baby;* avoidant—skip nine months—*Mother;* angry and disliking of contact) leads me to wish to clarify the obvious. The fact that avoidance on the part of a twelve-month-old baby is associated with anger and a dislike of physical contact on the part of the mother, subsequently *or* previously, offers no insight into who did what to whom. In this context, I have observed a newborn whose odd, perhaps reflexive behavior gave the impression that he was avoiding and rejecting his mother. Microanalysis of his mother's behavior suggested both that she responded to his behavior as though it were indeed rejection, and that from the first she was easily angered and disliking of contact. At two years the child avoided her in the strange situation.

The Ainsworth data show several of the avoidant babies exhibiting odd behaviors during the last quarters of the first year of life. In one baby there is staring; the baby appears to be "in a trance" at times; and the observer fears autistic tendencies. Another baby rocks; slaps his own face; pulls his ear; digs into his arm with his nails; and (by his mother's report) in the early months pulled out some of his hair. Another avoidant baby is described as rocking repeatedly in a stereotyped way; he has odd vocalizations (he "barks"); his face is devoid of affect; he seems attached to objects and the environment more than people. Another baby also lacks affect; becomes over-absorbed in objects; he "scratches" repeatedly on objects; and he too pulls his ears. Some of these odd behaviors are of the kind that occur in conflict situations. No doubt when the data are fully analyzed there will be a positive relation with avoidance, since nonavoidant babies do not show behaviors of this kind or do not show them to this degree.

While during the first months of life, the avoidant babies are fully as cuddly as the nonavoidant babies when held (Main & Ainsworth 1975) by the last quarter of the first year of life it is evident that there is a conflict centering in the infant-mother physical contact relationship. While those avoidant babies who have opportunity to do so initiate as many or even more contacts than other babies, they do not respond positively as other babies do when the mother initiates contact and holds them. When they are held they fail to sink in or cuddle and, unlike many other babies, they do not hold on tightly. Finally, the babies who will become avoidant in the strange situation spend a far higher proportion of their contacts with the mother and other persons in tentatively touching and patting them; and some tend to touch odd parts such as feet, shoes, and legs rather than touching the mother more centrally.

Work is also in progress on the Ainsworth data concerning the relationship between avoidance and angry behavior. No simple statement can be made regarding infant anger, since angry behavior occurs in such diverse forms and circumstances. It is certainly not only the avoidant babies who become angry, nor only the avoidant babies who have temper tantrums. Two of six strongly avoidant babies show little anger between nine and twelve months, yet several of the seemingly angriest babies in the sample are those who will become highly avoidant in the strange situation. This kind of thing is of course not unrelated to maternal behavior.

What in fact *best* distinguishes the to-become-avoidant babies' anger from others (over and above its apparent extremity) is the fact that aggressive expression is redirected or even appears out of context, and that this kind of thing happens only in the avoidant babies. An example of apparent redirection: the baby hits the mother's chair after she has left. An example of anger appearing out of context: the baby hits or bites his mother suddenly and for no ascertainable reason, perhaps while smiling and in the midst of play.

In my own study, I also assessed both aggressive and "odd" behavior. The "odd" behaviors appearing in my sample of thirty-eight twenty-one-month-old toddlers included: stereotypes; hand-flapping; echolalia; inappropriate affect (inexplicable fears, inappropriate laughter) and other behaviors appearing out of context. This set of behaviors related positively to avoidance of the mother nine months earlier.*

---

*There seemed no way of fully defining in advance a set of potential "conflict" behaviors, nor even a set of potential "odd" behaviors—yet to know which children showed this undefinable set seemed valuable. I therefore simply asked the "blind"

Angry behavior was assessed three times in my study. During the Bayley examination, the Bayley examiner rated the baby for the extent to which he had had a tantrum. "Tantrum" was positively related to avoidance, although the relation fell just short of conventional levels of significance ($r = .29$, $p<.10$).

During the Play Session video taped two weeks later, a tally was made for each child of the number of episodes of "nonexploratory hitting and banging": this had a positive relation to avoidance. We also tallied the number of times that the children hit, pinched, or otherwise directed angry behavior toward their mothers: this too was positively related to avoidance. Since each of these three different measures related positively to avoidance of the mother, there seems little doubt that the relationship exists within the sample. An impression now being examined is that the avoidant children were once again the ones whose "stimulus" for aggressive behavior was indiscernible.

In the Main study there were two opportunities to assess the toddlers' willingness to interact with persons other than the mother. These occurred when he was examined by the Bayley examiner, and during a playmate portion of the video taped play session when an adult woman playmate entered the room and invited the babies to participate in a game of ball.

During and following the Bayley examination, the Bayley examiner took careful note concerning the behavior of the toddler in interaction with herself. An assistant unaware of the Bayley score given each infant then rated the toddlers from this record, on two scales. The toddlers were rated first for their cooperation in taking the examination: cooperation related negatively to avoidance of the mother. The toddlers were also rated for the extent to which they showed a "game-like-spirit" in taking the test. A baby taking the test would show a game-like spirit to the extent that he treated the test as an opportunity to engage in playful interaction with the examiner. Game-like spirit was negatively related to avoidance of the mother.

During the playmate play portion of the play session we first simply asked whether the toddlers made a full, direct approach to

___

assistants to note each time that the toddler did anything which seemed odd to them, and a simple number of instances were tallied.

the playmate as she came in the door to invite them to a game of ball. "Approach" related negatively to avoidance. One strongly mother-avoidant infant (who had an excellent relationship with her father) approached the playmate directly. The other substantially avoidant babies who approached the playmate did so only abortively, turning away or spinning away, or (in one case) turning in a full circle and, with a strange little bow, putting hands to ears. Once the game of ball began, we tallied the number of times that the toddler returned the ball to the playmate in a game-like manner. This too related negatively to avoidance. During the entire twenty minutes that the playmate attempted to interact with the toddlers a tally was kept of the number of times that the toddlers showed gaze aversion or movements of physical avoidance: this tally of movements directed away from the playmate at twenty-one months was positively related to avoidance of the mother nine months previously.

These simple counts do not well enough express the difficulty of interacting with some (not all) of the mother-avoiding toddlers. One of the difficulties in interacting with these babies seems to center in a failure to provide facial feedback to the would-be-interacting partner. This is my impression, and needs substantiation. We are, therefore, presently rating toddlers (like mothers) for facial expressiveness and for pleasure shown in the face. In the meantime, we find that the number of instances in which the toddlers smiled or laughed about the toys is negatively related to avoidance of the mother. Analyses of the first ten-minute segments of the hour-long tape also show a negative relation between avoidance and number of utterances made by the baby and between avoidance and apparent looking directly into the mother's face.

Thus, we find in the mother-avoiding toddlers at twenty-one months both a consistent absence of positive social and affective behavior, angry behavior, and active withdrawal from the playmate. This relationship holds over the nine-month span between observations, despite the fact that the situations for observation differ greatly. The correlations computed between each of the above-mentioned social and affective behaviors and each of the five discrete attachment behaviors (crying, touching, looking, smiling, and vocalizing) are insignificant.

SUMMARY

This has been a long chapter. It is not a study of day-care, but a study of a behavior appearing in some day-care children, which, when appearing in home-reared children, is indicative of social and emotional disturbance. It can be summarized as follows:

1. This chapter introduces to those concerned with the development of children and their care a behavior not previously noted by researchers other than Ainsworth and her colleagues: that is, the child's avoidance of his mother as it appears following brief separations in a strange situation.

2. This behavior is of a type that appears in conflict situations.

3. This behavior seems theoretically expectable when attachment figures repeatedly behave in such a way as to elicit withdrawal from themselves, while at the same time they forbid approach.

4. On the part of the infant, avoidance has been shown related to angry behavior, to a set of odd behaviors, and to an unwillingness to interact even with persons other than the mother.

5. The anger of the avoidant baby is not directly expressed, neither in the reunion episodes of the strange situation (when, in contrast to some openly angry babies, the child looks away and moves away) nor in the normal interactive situation, where his anger often appears disordered, displaced, and unpredictable.

6. The mother of the avoidant infant appears angry, inexpressive, and disliking of physical contact with the infant.

7. Although infant avoidance is also related to ratings given mothers for "rejection" of the infant, no inference regarding the initial cause of the mother's rejection can yet be drawn; the mother may be responding to peculiar behavior in the baby.

8. While the Ainsworth measure of avoidance of the mother relates to the above maternal and infant behaviors seen outside of the strange situation, the conventionally used strange situation measures of "discrete attachment behaviors" do not.

9. According to Blehar (1974, and in this volume) avoidance of the mother in the strange situation appears more strongly in day-care than in home-reared children (p<.0005).

10. Although I believe avoidance of the attachment figure is very likely indicative of anger even in day-care two- and three-year-

olds, the difference in age and rearing condition may well qualify its meaning and sequelae (Douglass 1976). The home-reared one-year-old may be angry because of an interactive history, the day-care two- or three-year-old angry only because of one more unwonted separation—and anger based on distorted interaction may signal greater social and emotional disturbance than anger based on sensitivity to separation. The meaning of avoidance as it appears in these older day-care children is therefore not yet ascertained, but it is a matter for empirical investigation. The data and theory presented in the confines of this chapter, however, make that investigation not a luxury, but a requirement.

REFERENCES

Ainsworth, M. D. S. 1967. *Infancy in Uganda: Infant care and the growth of love.* Baltimore: Johns Hopkins University Press.

———. 1969. Object relations, dependency and attachment: a theoretical review of infant-mother relationship. *Child Development* 40: 969–1025.

———. Attachment and dependency: A comparison. In *Attachment and dependence,* J. L. Gewirtz (ed.) Washington, D.C.: Winston (distributed by John Wiley and Sons, New York).

———. 1973. The development of infant-mother attachment. In *Review of child development research,* B. Caldwell & H. Ricciuti, (eds.) vol. 3, Chicago: University of Chicago Press.

———. 1973. Anxious attachment and defensive reactions. Paper given at the biennial meeting of the Society for Research in Child Development, Philadelphia.

Ainsworth, M. D. S., & Bell, S. M. V. 1970. Attachment, exploration and separation: Illustrated by the behavior of one-year-olds in a strange situation. *Child Development* 41: 49–67.

Ainsworth, M. D. S., Bell, S. M. V., & Stayton, D. J. 1971. Individual differences in strange-situation behavior of one-year-olds. In *The origins of human social relations,* H. R. Schaffer (ed.) London: Academic Press, pp. 17–57.

Ainsworth, M. D. S., Blehar, M. C., Waters, E., & Wall, S. 1976. Strange-situation behavior of one-year-olds. Monograph in preparation.

Ainsworth, M. D. S., & Wittig, B. A. 1969. Attachment and exploration behavior of one-year-olds in a strange-situation. In *Determinants of Infant Behavior* 4, B. M. Foss, (ed.) London: Methuen.

Argyle, M., & Dean, J. 1975. Eye-contact, distance and affiliation. *Sociometry* 28: 289–304.

Bateson, G., Jackson, D., Haley, J., & Weakland, J. 1956. Toward a theory of schizophrenia. *Behavioral Science* I: 251–64.

Bell, S. M. V. 1970. The development of the concept of the object as related to infant-mother attachment. *Child Development* 41: 291–311.

Bertrand, M. 1969. *The behavioral repertoire of the stumptail macaque.* Basel and New York: Karger.

Blehar, M. C. 1974. Anxious attachment and defensive reactions associated with daycare, *Child Development* 45: 683–92.

Bowlby, J. 1958. The nature of the child's tie to his mother. *International Journal of Psychoanalysis* 39: 350.

———. 1969. Attachment, volume I of *Attachment and loss.* New York: Basic Books.

———. 1973. *Separation: Anxiety and anger.* Volume II of *Attachment and loss.* New York: Basic Books.

Brackbill, Y. 1958. Extinction of the smiling response in infants as a function of reinforcement schedule. *Child Development* 29: 115–24.

Brazelton, B., Koslowski, B., & Main, M. 1974. The origins of reciprocity: the early mother-infant interaction. In *The effect of the infant on its caregiver,* M. Lewis and L. Rosenblum (eds.) New York: John Wiley and Sons.

Bretherton, I., & Ainsworth, M. D. S. 1974. Responses of one-year-olds to a stranger in a strange-situation. In *Origins of behavior,* vol. 2, *Fear,* M. Lewis & L. Rosenblum (eds.) New York: John Wiley & Sons.

Bronson, G. W. 1972. Infants' reactions to unfamiliar persons and novel objects. *Monographs of the Society for Research in Child Development,* ser. no. 148, vol. 37, no. 3.

Burlingham, D., & Freud, A. 1944. *Infants without families,* London: Allen & Unwin.

Chance, M. R. A. 1962. An interpretation of some agonistic postures: the role of 'cut-off' acts and postures. *Symposium of the Zoological Society of London* 8: 71–89.

Coss, R. 1972. Reflections on the evil eye. *Human Behavior* 3: 17–22.

Darwin, C. 1972. *The voyage of the Beagle.* New York: Basic Books.

———. 1877. *Mind II,* p. 292.

Douglass, A. 1976. A study of parent-child interaction and infant attachment behavior in two blind couples with sighted infants. Honors thesis submitted to the Department of Psychology, University of California, Berkeley.

Eibl-Eiebesfeldt, I. 1970. *Ethology: The Biology of Behavior.* New York: Holt, Rinehart, and Winston. Translated by Erich Klinghammer.

Freud, A., & Burlingham, D. 1943. *War and children,* New York: Medical Warbooks.

Goodenough, F. L. 1932. Expressions of the emotions in a blind-deaf child. *Journal of Abnormal Social Psychology* 47: 328–33.

Hamburg, D. A., 1969. Observations of mother-infant interactions in primate field studies. In *Determinants of infant behavior, IV*, B. Foss (ed.), London: Methuen, pp. 3–14.

Hare, B. 1952. A comparative study of the reactions of a two-year-old child. Dissertation. University of London. Child Development Department.

Harlow, H. F. 1961. The development of affectional patterns in infant monkeys. In *Determinants of infant behavior, IV,* B. Foss (ed.), London: Methuen; New York: John Wiley & Sons, pp. 75–97.

Heinicke, C., & Westheimer, I. 1965. *Brief separations.* New York: International Universities Press.

Hinde, R. A. 1966. *Animal behavior: A synthesis of ethology and comparative psychology.* New York: McGraw-Hill.

Hutt, C., & Ounsted, C. 1966. The biological significance of gaze aversion with particular reference to the syndrome of infantile autism. *Behavioral Science* II: 346–56.

Kaufman, I. C., & Rosenblum, L. A. 1969. The waning of the mother-infant bond in two species of macaque. In *Determinants of infant behavior IV,* B. Foss (ed.). London: Methuen, pp. 37–59.

Kendon, A. 1967. Some functions of gaze-direction in social interaction. *Acta Psychology* 26: 22–63.

Main, M. 1973. Exploration, play and level of cognitive functioning as related to child-mother attachment. Dissertation, The Johns Hopkins University.

Main, M., & Ainsworth, M. D. S., Physical contact as a signal of security. Manuscript in preparation (1976).

Main, M., & Brazelton, T. B., Micro-ethology: detailed analysis of brief segments of behavior as a potential diagnostic tool. (To be submitted *Merrill-Palmer Quarterly*).

Main, M., & Waters, E., Autism and adaptation. Paper given at the third biennial conference of the International Society for the Study of Behavioral Development, Surrey, England, July 1975.

Medawar, P. B. 1967. *The art of the soluble.* London: Methuen.

Meehl, P. E. 1962. Schizotaxia, schizotypy, schizophrenia. *American Psychologist* 17: 827–38.

Prugh, D. G., Staub, E. M., Sands, H., Kieschbaum, R. M., & Lenihan, E. A. 1953. A study of the emotional reactions of children and families to hospitalization and illness. *American Journal of Ortho-psychiatry* 23: 70.

Rheingold, H. L., Gewirtz, J. L., & Ross, H. W. 1959. Social conditioning of vocalizations in the infant. *Journal of Comparative and Physiological Psychology* 52: 68–73.

Riemer, M. D. 1949. The averted gaze. *Psychiatric Quarterly* pp. 108–115.

Robertson, J. 1953. Some responses of young children to the loss of maternal care. *Nursing Times* 49: 382.

Robertson, J., & Bowlby, J. 1952. Responses of young children to separation from their mothers. *Courr. Cent. Int. Enf.* 2: 131–42.

Robertson, J., & Robertson, J. 1971. Young children in brief separations. *Psychoanalytic Study of the Child* 26: 264–315.

Robson, K. S. 1967. The role of eye-to-eye contact in maternal-infant attachment. *Journal of Child Psychology and Psychiatry* 8: 13–26.

Rosenblum, L. A., & Harlow, H. F. 1963. Approach-avoidance conflict in the mother-surrougate situation. *Psychological Reports* 12: 38–85.

Sackett, G., Griffin, G. A., Pratt, C., Joslyn, W. D., & Ruppenthal, G. 1967. Mother-infant and adult female choice behavior in rhesus monkeys after various rearing experiences. *J. Comp Physiol. Psychol.* 63: 376–81.

Schaffer, H. R., & Callender, M. A. 1959. Psychological effects of hospitalization in infancy. *Pediatrics* 24: 528–39.

Spencer-Booth, Y., & Hinde, R. A. 1971. Effects of brief separations from mothers during infancy on behavior of rhesus monkeys 6–24 months later. *Journal of Child Psychiatry and Allied Disciplines* 12(3): 157–72.

———. 1966. The effects of separating rhesus monkey infants from their mothers for six days. *Journal of Child Psychology and Psychiatry* 1: 179–98.

Sroufe, L. A., Waters, E. & Matas, L. 1974. Contextual determinants of infant affective response. In *The origins of behavior,* II, *Fear.* New York: John Wiley and Sons, pp. 49–72.

Stechler, G., & Latz, E. 1966. Some observations on attention and arousal in the human infant. *American Academy of Child Psychiatry.* 5: 517–25.

Stern, D., A micro-analysis of mother-infant interaction: behavior regulating social contact between a mother and her 3 1/2 month old twins. *Journal of the American Academy of Child Psychiatry,* 1971, *10,* 501–517.

———. Mother and infant at play: the dyadic interaction: involving facial, vocal and gaze behaviors. In *The Origins of Behavior,* M. Lewis and L. Rosenblum (eds.) New York: John Wiley and Sons, Vol. 1, 1973.

Tinbergen, N. 1974. A conversation with Nobel Prize Winner, Niko Tinbergen by Elizabeth Hall. *Psychology Today,* March 1974, pp. 65–80.

————. 1974. Ethology and stress diseases. *Science* 185: 20–27.

Tolan, W. 1975. Maternal facial expression as related to the child-mother attachment. Honors thesis submitted to the Department of Psychology, University of California, Berkeley.

Tomasini, L. 1975. Maternal behavior during a play session at 21 months as related to infant security of attachment. Honors thesis submitted to the Department of Psychology, University of California, Berkeley.

Vine, I. 1970. Communication by facial-visual signals. In *Social behavior in birds and mammal: Essays in the social ethology of animals and man.* John H. Crook (ed.). London: Academic Press.

Waters, E., Matas, L., & Sroufe, L. A. 1975. Infants' reactions to an approaching stranger: description validation and functional significance of wariness. *Child Development.*

Waters, E., & Main, M. An approach to avoidance through interval scaling. (In preparation.)

Watson, J. S. 1970. Smiling, cooing, and 'the game'. Paper given at the annual meeting of the American Psychological Association at Miami Beach.

3

SOCIAL AND INTELLECTUAL CONSEQUENCES OF DAY-CARE FOR HIGH-RISK INFANTS

Craig T. Ramey and Pamela J. Mills

When one reviews the literature on the development of impoverished children, evidence of deficits in function is abundant. Children who live in deprived environments, as defined by economic and educational level of parents, tend to be deficient on many of the general intellectual, cognitive and verbal measures of ability. Not all children from poor families, however, are considered to be at risk for developmental retardation. Even though persons who live in economically underprivileged environments evidence developmental retardation disproportionally (Deutsch & Brown 1964), there are many who function in the average or above average range of intelligence and who successfully achieve in the adult world. But there is a fundamental difference between poor children who perform adequately and those who do not.

Golden and Birns (1968) report "striking differences in cognitive and personality functioning between older preschool children from stable, low-income families and those from impoverished, socially disorganized families (p. 139)." Golden and Birns attributed these differences to gross variations in child-rearing practices. The children from stable, low-income families were found to profit more from preschool enrichment programs than were children from socially disorganized families. The children in the latter group already manifested serious learning problems at age three when they entered a preschool program.

Early experiences in chaotic and disorganized homes is considered by many to be one predominant contributing factor to the functional retardation and learning difficulties experienced by many children in our country today. Meier et al. (1970) report that "more than two-thirds of the 'slow learners' and 'school failures' are retarded on the basis of experiential deprivations which have left their scars before the child enters school (p. 408)." Heber (1971) identified a number of environmental variables, including maternal IQ, as good indicators of whether or not a child would function at a retarded level. Meier (1972) reported that certain groups of disadvantaged children, particularly those whose mothers had an IQ below 75, showed a steady decline in IQ from a normal level at age three to the retarded levels of their mothers.

Other aspects of the home environment that have been found related with reduced levels of functioning in children include low educational achievement of either or both parents, the absence of the father from the home, or the father's unstable work record in unskilled or semi-skilled labor. These factors, combined with low maternal intelligence and economic deprivation, increase the likelihood that offspring will function in the retarded range. While many of these facts are open to a genetic, as well as environmental, interpretation, the findings point to several avenues of intervention that might influence the development of high-risk children in a favorable direction.

Some external support systems have proven successful in effecting change in children who would be likely to function at a retarded level (Stedman et al. 1972). In effect, environmental manipulations can alter the course of intellectual development. Programs have attempted to offset the disadvantages of maternal separation and give the added cognitive and social input which the extreme lower-class home is frequently unable to provide.

Early intervention into the lives of potentially unsuccessful children has taken a variety of forms. Strategies have included day-care center programs in which either the child alone or the child and his mother were the target of change. Home-care programs in which the child, the mother, or the mother working with her child have also received major attention. Evaluation of these diverse intervention programs has been restricted in scope, however, with the focus being primarily on the cognitive gains which can be assessed by standardized measures of intelligence. The areas of social and emotional growth have been evaluated less frequently. Stedman et al. (1972) singled out the "lack of understanding of the affective domain (p. 38)" as the most significant gap in this area of knowledge.

INTERVENTION IMPACT ON THE FAMILY

One of the major gaps in research in the area of early childhood intervention is the impact of that intervention on the family as a unit. The child's relation to other family members, especially the mother, is obviously understudied. Most of the information available in this area is from home-centered intervention programs which have focused their attention on the mother or on the mother working with her child.

Involving the parents in the child's program is reported to have positive effects on the parents and other siblings, as well as on the target child's cognitive performance. Parents' own self-esteem and feelings of self-worth may have been enhanced by working with their own children. Parents hired as staff have shown positive changes on the variables tested. Some reports also indicate that the positive effects have been reflected in the achievement of their children (Social Research Group 1971). Reports have been made that there appears to be a correlation, if not a causal relationship, between the amount of parent participation and the cognitive gains of the children (Stearns, Search, & Rosenfeld 1971).

The effect of diffusion to other members of the family or neighborhood has been discussed as a positive effect of early intervention. Klaus and Gray (1968) reported that a home program had equal positive effects with a preschool program, plus had the added benefit of vertical diffusion to younger children and horizontal diffusion through the neighborhood.

Gordon (1969) used paraprofessionals to train parents to teach their own infants during the first year of life. An assessment at twelve months of age, using the Griffith Mental Scales, showed a significant difference between the experimental and untreated control groups. In addition, Gordon reports positive effects on parents' feelings of self-esteem and self-worth. Gutelius et al. (1972)

attribute a large part of the success of their program to an increased feeling of personal worth and self-confidence built up in the mother, with resulting change' in the mother-child relationship.

In a program designed to stimulate the child's language development, Levenstein (1970) had "toy demonstrators" go into the home and teach mothers verbally to interact with their children. Results from this study point to a mean IQ gain in the children of approximately 17 points—from an IQ of 85 to 102. A study by Karnes, Teska, Hodgins, and Badger (1970), in which the mother was provided training, endeavored to "prevent the inadequate cognitive and linguistic development characteristic of the disadvantaged child." On the Stanford-Binet, experimentals showed a 16 point advantage over controls and a 28 point advantage over siblings.

As noted before, Stedman et al. (1972), in their review of day-care and home-based educational intervention programs, discuss the inadequacy of such programs in delineating the social effects involved. They identify methodological and measurement weaknesses inhibiting accurate social assessment. They state that, although most intervention personnel believe that their programs have both long- and short-term social effects, there are few hard data to support this contention. Most of the data are subjective, yet clearly suggest an increase in family cohesiveness and a diffusion effect from participating children to siblings, parents and neighbors.

Because day-care intervention that does not involve the mother separates the mother and child for long periods of time during the day, serious ethical and theoretical considerations need to be addressed. Since the early social relationship between a mother and her infant is thought to be crucial for the child's subsequent development (see, for example, Ainsworth 1969), possible alteration of this early relationship is a serious social issue.

Caldwell, Wright, Honig, and Tannenbaum (1970) compared a group of thirty-month-old children who had been enrolled at a day-care center from approximately one year of age with a group of children who had not attended such a program. Three types of data were analyzed: (1) maternal interviews designed to gather information about attachment (2) an inventory of home stimulation and (3) Stanford–Binet or Cattell Infant Intelligence Scale results. The results indicated that the two groups of children did not differ in their degree of attachment to their mother.

More recently Blehar (in this volume) compared the attachment behaviors of twenty middle-class children attending day-care with twenty children who were being reared at home by their mothers. Half of the children in both groups were approximately two years old and half were approximately three years old. Most of the day-care children in both age groups had attended their day-care centers for less than six months.

Blehar used Caldwell's Inventory of Home Stimulation and Ainsworth's (1969) episodic strange situation. The day-care and home reared groups did not differ on any of the sub-scales of the Home Stimulation Inventory.

In general, behavior in the strange situation indicated that few differences exist at the two-year-old level; however, the three-year-old day-care attending children indicated more frequent behaviors which are taken as indices of attachment. For example, they maintain closer proximity to their mothers, engage in more crying upon separation, search more for their mothers upon the mothers' departure, and make fewer contacts with strangers during later separation episodes, after initially making more contacts.

As both Caldwell et al. (1970) and Blehar (this volume) note, there are several methodological limitations of their studies which may limit the generality of their findings. Most importantly, both investigators point out that random assignment to groups was not feasible. Thus, the extent to which day-care resulted in differing patterns of attachment must rest upon the assumption that the mother's decision to put her child into day-care or not does not reflect basic orientations toward children which would have resulted in differing attachment propensities independently of day-care placement.

In comparing her results which are discrepant from those of Caldwell et al. Blehar notes that "children accustomed to group-care from infancy (as Caldwell et al.'s sample was) may not experience the same overt disruption of the relationship with the mother as do children shifted from home-care to day-care at age two or three."

The study to be reported in this chapter was conceived as a beginning effort to specify some of the social and intellectual consequences of day-care that begins in the first quarter of the first year of life.

THE CAROLINA ABECEDARIAN PROJECT

In the fall of 1972, the Carolina Abecedarian Project was begun as an attempt to bring together a multidisciplinary team of researchers which would address itself both to demonstrating that developmental retardation could be prevented and to examining how various psychological and biological processes were affected by such preventive attempts. In the next few pages a general overview of the project will be presented to provide a background for the specific study to be discussed in this chapter.

Selection of Subjects for the Carolina Abecedarian Project

North Carolina Memorial Hospital, the University of North Carolina's teaching hospital, is the primary referral source for potential subjects for the project. Through its various prenatal clinics pass most of the expectant mothers of Orange County who are likely to meet the criteria for inclusion into our sample. All prenatal charts for mothers who are likely to have children who would qualify for the project are screened. In addition, liaison is maintained with the Orange County Department of Social Services and other community agencies which are likely to have contact with potentially eligible families.

Once a family is identified as being potentially eligible and has been referred, the supervisor of the project's infant nursery establishes contact with that family and arranges to see them at their home to explain the project and to determine if they are interested in participating, if invited to do so. During this interview the supervisor informs the parents that the Frank Porter Graham Center is conducting a long-term study on how children from economically limited families grow and develop during infancy and early childhood. She explains that the goal of this program is to find out what things make a baby a healthy and competent child. The supervisor further explains that the study consists of two separate programs. The first program (the control group) involves the periodic assessment of the child and other family members, especially the mother. Participation in this program includes the receipt of free formula, medical care, and disposable diapers. The second program (the experimental group) receives day-care services. It is explained that all mothers will be paid for the time that they spend in any of the assessment sessions either at the FPG Center or in their homes. Further, all transportation to and from the center is provided for the experimental group daily and for both groups whenever assessments are scheduled and the parents cannot transport themselves. The supervisor also informs the families that they will be assigned to one program or the other after the baby has been born and the sex determined.

If the supervisor determines that the family potentially meets the criteria for inclusion into the program, the expectant mother is invited to the Frank Porter Graham Child Development Center, where the project is being conducted, for a series of interviews. These interviews are designed to assess her attitudes toward child-rearing practices, to gather detailed family background information, to assess the mother's IQ, and to collect demographic information about the family.

One purpose of these interviews is to rate the family on an experimental version "high-risk index" which is shown in Table 3.1. This index was constructed before beginning the Abecedarian Project. Weights were assigned to the various factors based upon our "best guess" of their relative importance. Because there was and is little epidemiological data concerning the factors linked to developmental retardation it was impossible to assign empirically derived weights to each factor. However, it is hoped that as the sample families are followed it will be possible to derive empirical weights through multiple regression analyses which can be used to predict developmental status in future samples more precisely.

After target children are born, qualifying families are pair-matched on sex of the child, maternal IQ, number of siblings, and high-risk index scores, and are randomly assigned to either the experimental or the control group. To date, fifty-nine families have been offered membership in either the experimental or control groups and fifty-eight have accepted. All families remain in the program except two, each of whose infant died in the first year of life. One child who died was diagnosed as a "crib-death" and the other child died from heart failure secondary to endocardial fibro-

Table 3.1. High-Risk Index

Mother's educational level (last grade completed)	Weights	Father's educational level (last grade completed)	Weights	Family income	Weights
6	8	6	8	1,000	8
7	7	7	7	1,001–2,000	7
8	6	8	6	2,001–3,000	6
9	3	9	3	3,001–4,000	5
10	2	10	2	4,001–5,000	4
11	1	11	1	5,001–6,000	0
12	0	12	0		

Other Indications of High-Risk and Point Values

Pts.
3   1. Father absent for reasons other than health or death.
3   2. Absence of maternal relatives in local area (i.e., parents, grandparents, or brothers or sisters of majority age).
3   3. Siblings of school age who are one or more grades behind age-appropriate grade or who score equivalently low on school administered achievement tests.
3   4. Payments received from welfare agencies within past three years.
3   5. Record of father's work indicates unstable and unskilled or semi-skilled labor.
3   6. Records of mother's or father's IQ indicates scores of 90 or below.
3   7. Records of sibling's IQ indicates scores of 90 or below.
3   8. Relevant social agencies in the community indicate that the family is in need of assistance.
1   9. One or more members of the family has sought counseling or professional help in the past three years.
1   10. Special circumstances not included in any of the above which are likely contributors to cultural or social disadvantage.

(Criterion for inclusion in high-risk sample is a score 11.

elastosis, a disease which is particularly difficult to detect at birth. One child had been in the experimental group and one child had been in the control group.

Both the experimental and the control subjects receive the following services:

1. Family support social work services: On a request basis from the parents and from routine visits to all families, the Abecedarian Project seeks to provide all families with goods, services, or guidance in such areas as legal help, family planning, obtaining food, obtaining clothing, or any other services which will help to keep the families intact. However, no advice is given to any of the families

concerning how they treat or interact with their children. The only exception to this procedure is that advice and treatment is given concerning medical and routine physical care.

2. Nutritional supplements: Each child in the experimental group receives the bulk of his nutrition at the day-care center. Breakfast, lunch, and an afternoon snack are served each day. To control for nutrition as one explanatory variable in observed differences between the experimental and control groups, the control group receives free formula on an unlimited basis for as long as the children use it, and plans are underway to provide other nutritional supplements in the second year of life.

3. Medical care: All medical care for the center-attending children is provided by the Frank Porter Graham Center medical staff. Free medical care for the control children is provided by the Frank Porter Graham staff and two University-affiliated clinics. Thus, all children have available adequate medical care, and the project maintains records on all care delivered.

4. Transportation: Transportation to and from the Center is provided for all subjects participating in the project.

5. Payment for participation: All mothers are paid for participating in psychological evaluations.

6. Disposable diapers are provided free to the control subjects as an inducement for continuing participation.

The experimental group differs from the control group in that the former receives a planned curriculum administered throughout the day. The day-care component of the Center operates from 7:45 A.M. to 5:30 P.M. each weekday. A schedule for the youngest infants is presented in Table 3.2. Infants are admitted to the day-care group when they are between one and three months of age. The nursery for children under one year of age typically contains fourteen children and five teachers.

Population and Sample for the Present Study

The subjects for this study were sixty infants and their mothers representing three groups. The first two groups were comprised of the first high-risk participants of the Frank Porter Graham Child

Table 3.2. Sample Daily Routine for Four-week to One-year Olds

A.M.			
7:30	Arrival of children. Each child is greeted individually and parents are talked with. All children are changed and allowed a free play period within the large group.	12:00	Nap time. Staff members eat lunch.
		NOON	Short staff meetings occasionally.
9:00	Children are divided into groups; teachers play with groups.	P.M.	
		12:30	Teachers maintain daily records for each child. Accomplishments, emerging interests, etc., are recorded in short narrative form.
10:00	Curriculum items, such as perceptual or motor training.		
10:30	Nap time for the youngest infants. One-to-one game playing for the older infants. The "talking game," "Peek-a-boo," and other games used to provide contingency and object permanence awareness.	1:30	Individual attention for awake children.
		2:30	All children gradually awakened.
		3:00	Floor play or outdoor play.
		4:00	Children begin to leave.
11:00	Change, clean-up, and serve lunch.	4:30	Individual play with remaining infants. Staff members begin to leave.
11:30	Lunch continued.		
		5:15	All children picked up by parents or taken home.

Development Center's Abecedarian Project. High-Risk Experimental (HRE) consisted of fifteen mother-infant dyads representing the day-care component, and High-Risk Control (HRC) consisted of fifteen mother-infant dyads, representing the home-control sample. The third group consisted of thirty mother-infant dyads representing a stratified sample of the general population (GPS) and selected at random from the birth records for the local community.

The high-risk groups were matched on the variables of age of infant, sex, race, socioeconomic status, number of siblings, and mother's measured intelligence. The group representing the general population was matched to the high-risk groups on age and sex of infant and live birth parity. The infants in all three groups ranged from 3½ to 9½ months of age, with a mean age of approximately 200 days.

A personal interview and observation of the General Population Sample were used to eliminate infants with obvious physical abnormalities that might have negated normal mother-infant interaction. Also, only mothers in the United States were included for study.

Recruitment of general population sample. Mothers were contacted by telephone, whenever possible, and invited to participate in a study to determine the activity levels of young children in the presence of their mothers. The mothers were told that the study would require approximately 2½ to 3 hours of their time, that they would be paid $5.00 for their involvement and that transportation to the Center would be provided if desired.

During the initial contact, a time was arranged for the interviewer to visit in the home. A time was scheduled when the child would normally be awake and active, and the mother would have approximately 1½ hours to spend with the interviewer.

None of the mothers representing the high-risk groups refused to participate, while only three mothers representing the general population refused.

Table 3.3 presents the demographic characteristics of the families included in the study.

Table 3.3. Selected Characteristics of the High-Risk Groups Compared with the General Population Sample

Characteristic	High-risk	General
Number of families	30	30
Race of families	100% Black	20% Black
Age of child (average)	6.5 months	6.6 months
Percent male	33%	33%
Percent first born	50%	50%
Percent breast fed	3.3%	36.7%
Age of mother (average)	22.20 years	27.33 years
Mother's education (percentage of persons)		
1–8 years	3.3%	3.3%
9–11 years	63.3%	3.3%
High school graduate	33.3%	10%
13–15 years	0%	23.3%
College graduate	0%	30%
Graduate education	0%	30%
Father's education (average)	10th grade	College graduate*
Family income (average)	$1,500 yearly	$10,780 yearly

*70 percent of the general population fathers had graduate education.

High-risk rating. Since participation in the Abecedarian Project is restricted to families identified as being "at risk" of having developmentally retarded children, the high-risk rating of the families representing the general population sample was determined. Although it was impractical to determine the IQ level of members of the general population, the families were assessed according to the remaining items on the High-Risk Index.

Excluding the points possible for low intelligence on the part of the mother, father or siblings, the Abecedarian high-risk families had a mean score of 18.5. (As noted previously, inclusion in the project is limited to families scoring 11 or more points.) The families representing the general population had a mean score of 6.6. Two families scored at the high-risk level (one at 17 points and one at 11 points), while five families earned zero (0) points. Sixteen of the families in the GPS earned points on the High-Risk Index only by having no maternal relatives living in the local area.

Instrumentation

HOME. In addition to gathering information concerning the demographic characteristics and high-risk ratings of the families, part of the time in the home was spent conducting Caldwell's Home Observation for Measurement of the Environment (HOME), an Inventory of Infants (1968). This observation and interview inventory was used to assess the factors of maternal warmth, the absence of punishment and hostility, the organization of the physical and temporal environment, the appropriateness of toys provided, maternal involvement and the opportunity for variety in daily stimulation. These factors, ordered as to their importance, represent "certain aspects of the quantity and quality of social, emotional and cognitive support available to a young child (birth to three years) within his home" (Instruction Manual).

One-third of the forty-three items were obtained through talking with the mother and two-thirds were obtained through actual observation. Interobserver reliability for the HOME was based upon independent scoring of each item of the same interviews by three raters. An overall 93.6 percent agreement was achieved.

Rotter. A measure of locus of control, Rotter's (1966) Internality-Externality Scale (I–E), was given to all mothers. Statements were presented orally in pairs and mothers were asked to choose the statement they agreed with more. Their choices are thought to represent values and attitudes parents might transmit to their children.

PARI. In addition to the I–E Scale, another measure was administered. The Parental Attitude Research Instrument (PARI) developed by Schaefer and Bell (1958) and modified by Emmerich (1969) was presented orally. The mothers were asked to designate their degree of agreement or disagreement to a series of statements. These statements represented eleven scales with substantial loadings on three factors: Authoritarian Control (five scales), Hostility—Rejection (three scales), and Democratic Attitudes (three scales).

Bayley. The Bayley Scales of Infant Development (BSID) were administered to all infants. Both the Mental Development Index and the Psychomotor Development Index were obtained. These two scales were given to the infants to ascertain their developmental status. In order to assure an optimal and equal setting, the Bayley was administered during a visit to the Center. The high-risk children had been in the testing setting at 3, 6, and 9 months if they were that old. The experimental and control groups had been tested equally often. The Bayley Scales were probably administered for the first time to the General Population Sample during this study. Interrater item reliability based upon independent assessment of the same children by two trained persons was 91 percent.

Mother-infant interaction. Specific behaviors of the mother and infant were assessed in a controlled naturalistic environment similar to the one used by Lewis and Goldberg (1969). A twenty-five-minute video tape was made of the interaction between mother and infant in a room furnished with comfortable, home-like furniture. All infants and mothers in this study had never been in this situation before and therefore, they were in a novel setting. Available within the room were a crib and toys for the child and a television and current magazines for the mother. The mothers were informed that this part of the study was being conducted to determine the activity level of babies when they were with their mothers in a new and different setting.

Mother-Infant Interaction: Procedure of Taping

1. On the day of taping, the mother and infant were escorted into the observation room. The videocamera and microphone were pointed out to the mother, and she was told we were taping so that we could analyze the data at a later date.

2. The television and magazines were pointed out, and the mother was told that she should respond to the child's needs as she would at home. The currency and type of magazines were manipulated to allow for positive valence and as an attempt at a controlled naturalistic observation.

3. The mother-infant dyad was taped for twenty-five minutes.

Categories of behavior. Behavior was recorded into Esterline Angus Event records for each of the following categories. Both frequency and duration were recorded.

Mother

Talk to Child: Any vocalization made by mother that was directed toward child.

Touch Child: Any physical contact to mother toward child, including responses by mother which were child-care oriented e.g., wiping nose, helping child to sit up. Holding child was not considered to be touching.

Hold Child: Mother had child in arms or on lap, supporting weight of child.

Demonstrate Toys: Any time mother demonstrated toy to child, including winding toy, listening to or talking about toy to child, thumbing through book if not actually reading to child.

Interact with Child without Toys: Any reciprocal interaction* between mother and child that did not involve a nonsocial

---

Reciprocal Interaction: Mutual involvement of both mother and child as measured by overt and/or attending behavior.

object. It might have included actual touch, but touch was not required.

Read to Self: Any time mother read to herself.

Read to Child: Any time mother read to child from book or magazine.

Television On: Any time television set was turned on, regardless of whether or not child or mother was watching

Child

Vocalizes: Any non-fussy vocal sounds by child.

Fuss/Cry: Any fussy noise-making or cry by child, including vocalizations of protest.

Play with Toys: Anytime child manipulated or attended to pre-specified object, including actually touching toys, plus watching or attending to toys.

Interact with Mother and Toys: Any time child and mother were playing together and a nonsocial object was involved. Child was playing with toy and mother or attending to mother's involvement with toy. It involved reciprocal interaction of mother and child.

On Furniture: Any time child was on furniture, which included a sofa and chair. It also included mother's sitting in chair and holding child on lap.

In Crib: Any time child was in infant crib.

Feeding/Sleeping: Any time child was drinking, eating, or sleeping. Included were times child was not moving arms, legs, and head, whether or not observer could tell if child were actually sleeping.

Interaction reliability. Interobserver reliability was based upon independent scorings by three trained observers. Prior to beginning the study, categories of behavior were discussed and operational definitions were determined. Practice tapes were scored, coding the behavior for both mother and infant.

Four complete sessions were checked for reliability, one for each high-risk group and two for the general population (one out of fifteen). Random ten-minute tape segments were coded for both mother and infant, scoring one out of every five tapes. Three ten-minute segments of both mother and infant behavior were coded for each high-risk group and six ten-minute segments for the general population sample. (Twenty percent of the tapes in each group were checked for reliability.)

Mean interobserver reliability across categories for the three observers was 95.6 percent, with a range from 91 percent to 100 percent.

Results

Developmental status of infants. Scores on the Bayley Scales of Infant Development (BSID) were analyzed, using the multivariate analysis of variance (MANOVA) technique. Table 3.4 presents by groups, the means and standard deviations for both mental (MDI) and psychomotor (PDI) indices.

The results of the MANOVA analysis are presented in Table 3.5. A breakdown by scales using univariate F tests indicates significant differences among groups on the PDI (p < .02), but not on the MDI (p < .285).

HRC vs. GPS. In order to ascertain differences between the high-risk home-reared and the general-population infants, a between-groups comparison was made. Results indicated a significant multivariate F (F mult$_{2,56}$ = 4.093, p < .022). Univariate F tests revealed significant differences on the PDI (F$_{1,57}$ = 8.152, p < .006) with the general population sample scoring 12.57 points higher than the high-risk control group. The MDI results did not indicate significant differences.

Table 3.4. Means and Standard Deviations of MDI and PDI

GROUP		MDI	PDI
HRE	M	109.000	106.933
	SD	13.522	10.747
HRC	M	100.933	96.667
	SD	10.250	12.494
GPS	M	105.200	109.233
	SD	15.356	15.800

Table 3.5. MANOVA for Bayley Scales of Infant Development

Multivariate F Tests				
Tests of Roots	F	DFHYP	DFERR	p
1 through 2	2.401	4.000	112.000	0.054
2 through 2	1.529	1.000	56.500	0.221

Univariate F Tests			
	F (2.57)	Mean SQ	p
MDI	1.282	244.415	0.285
PDI	4.180	809.671	0.020

HRE vs. HRC. Comparison between the two high-risk groups on the Bayley Scales demonstrated a significant difference on the psychomotor (PDI) measure only. The high-risk day-care group scored 10.27 points higher than the home-reared infants ($F_{1,57} = 4.081$, p < .048).

Thus, the Bayley tests revealed that both the center-attending high-risk infants (HRE) and the general-population infants (GPS) scored significantly higher on the PDI than did the home-reared high-risk infants (HRC). Also, although not significantly different, both HRE and GPS scored higher than the HRC on the MDI. It is obvious from Table 3.4 that the HRE and GPS do not differ significantly from one another. Thus, the experimental group is equal in performance to the general population and both groups scored significantly above the control group with scores that are above national norms.

Mother-Infant Interaction Data Results

Duration of behavior. Mean comparisons on fifteen criterion variables (duration of behavior) across three groups again involved using the multivariate analysis of variance technique. Duration of behavior in each category was used as the lowest level of data analysis, using time accumulation during the twenty-five-minute taping session.

Table 3.6 presents, by groups, the means and standard deviations of each category of behavior coded for the infants.

Table 3.6. Means and Standard Deviations of Time in Seconds of Categories of Infants Behavior in Mother-Infant Interaction Observation

GROUP		Sleep	Child voc.	In crib	Child play	Int M&Toys	On furn	Fuss/ Cry
HRE	M	58.267	136.333	14.467	413.067	540.467	71.000	68.600
	SD	161.307	86.685	56.029	350.282	253.378	182.802	98.263
HRC	M	104.533	71.467	26.333	547.333	303.200	263.800	145.800
	SD	185.310	85.652	77.099	437.924	310.040	404.142	150.367
GPS	M	99.000	113.333	74.167	519.067	498.567	98.733	94.600
	SD	213.810	85.479	199.221	439.641	342.321	210.042	156.711

Table 3.7 presents, by groups, the means and standard deviations for the *mother*'s behavior.

Multivariate comparison of all three groups simultaneously. The mother-infant interaction data were analyzed to determine the significance of overall differences among the groups for both mothers and infants in the same analysis. In order to determine which categories contributed to the overall difference, univariate F tests were used. Due to the large variances on most variables, square root transformations of scores were employed.

Univariate F tests revealed significant differences among groups in the behaviors of child vocalization ($F_{2,57} = 3.621$, $p < .033$); child interacts with mother and toys ($F_{2,57} = 4.523$ $p < .015$); mother talks to child ($F_{2,57} = 6.931$, $p < .002$); mother reads to

Table 3.7. Means and Standard Deviations of Time in Seconds of Categories of Mothers' Behavior in Mother-Infant Interaction Observation

GROUP		Dem toy	Mat talk	TV on	Read child	Read self	Touch	Hold	Int no toys
HRE	M	522.867	232.933	365.134	0.0	266.133	350.467	238.600	103.267
	SD	303.139	206.234	629.758	0.0	336.162	396.717	344.352	145.410
HRC	M	447.800	140.867	363.067	0.0	241.333	260.267	224.533	10.133
	SD	281.926	137.754	628.639	0.0	414.788	384.454	404.704	23.099
GPS	M	575.467	331.400	102.700	18.767	176.200	169.133	266.200	42.867
	SD	352.855	192.299	303.112	35.052	269.929	174.168	342.556	68.200

child ($F_{2,57} = 4.814$, p < .012); and mother interacts with child without toys ($F_{2,57} = 3.414$, p < .040); but exact location of differences was not identified. Special contrast analyses were used to identify group differences.

HRC vs. GPS. Significant differences were found in favor of the GPS in the areas of child vocalization ($F_{1,57} = 4.498$, p < .038); child interacts with mother and toys ($F_{1,57} = 6.305$, p < .015); mother talks to child ($F_{1,57} = 13.414$, p < .001); and mother reads to child ($F_{1,57} = 6.419$, p < .014).

HRE vs. GPS. Special contrast comparisons between the high-risk day-care group and the general population sample identified only one difference was in the behavior of mother reads to child ($F_{1,57} = 6.419$, p < .014). The means indicated that GPS mothers read to their infants more than HRE mothers. Thus, except for this one variable the experimental group and the general population group appear quite comparable.

HRE vs. HRC. Comparison between the high-risk center-attending and the high-risk home-reared infants demonstrated differences favoring the day-care group. The two high-risk groups showed significant differences in the areas of child vocalization ($F_{1,57} = 6.641$, p < .013); child interacts with mother and toys ($F_{1,57} = 7.848$, p < .007); and mother interacts with child without toys ($F_{1,57} = 6.775$, p < .012). On each of these variables the HRE scored significantly higher than did the HRC.

Frequency of simultaneous behavior. Another level of analysis of the interaction data involved a comparison among groups using frequency of occurrence of behavior. Utilizing a ten-second unit of time, behaviors were coded as to their simultaneous occurrence. Mean comparisons on multiple measures across the three groups for each pairing of mother and infant behaviors identified differences that were not discernible in the analyses involving duration summaries.

Multivariate comparison of behavioral pairings for all three groups simultaneously. Table 3.8 identifies the simultaneous behavioral pairings that were significant at less than the .05 level when all three groups were compared.

Table 3.8. Behavior Pairings Significant across Three Groups

Behavioral pairings (mother/infant)	p
Demonstrate toys/play	0.012
Talk/vocalize	0.045
Talk/interact w/M & toys	0.006
Read/fuss	0.008

HRC vs. GPS: Behavioral pairings. Comparison between the high-risk control and general-population samples demonstrated significant differences on several pairings. The GPS mothers were found to demonstrate toys more while their infants were vocalizing (DemVoc $F_{1,57}$ = 5.027, p < .029); to have their infants interact with them more while the mothers were demonstrating toys (DemInt $F_{1,57}$ = 4.677, p < .035); to have the infants vocalize more while the mothers were talking (TalkVoc $F_{1,57}$ = 6.551, p < .013); and to have the infants interacting with the mothers with toys while the mothers were talking (TalkInt $F_{1,57}$ = 10.143, p < .002).

The HRC mothers were found to read more to themselves while their infants fussed (ReadAlone-Fuss $F_{1,57}$ = 9.381, p < .003).

HRE vs. GPS: Behavioral pairing. When comparing the high-risk day-care group with the general population, only two significant pairings were found. These results identified the GPS mothers as demonstrating toys more while their infants played alone (DemPlay $F_{1,57}$ = 4.183, p < .045) and as talking more while their infants played alone (TalkPlay $F_{1,57}$ = 5.145, p < .027).

HRE vs. HRC: Behavioral pairing. The two high-risk groups were found to differ significantly on five behavioral pairings. The home-reared high-risk infants played alone more while their mothers demonstrated toys (DemPlay $F_{1,57}$ = 9.479, p < .003) and fussed more while their mothers read to themselves (ReadAlone-Fuss $F_{1,57}$ = 6.929, p < .011). The center attending high-risk infants vocalized more while their mothers interacted with them without toys (IntW/OVoc $F_{1,57}$ = 6.036, p < .017).

Since the maternal behavior "interacts with child without toys" requires a reciprocal reaction on the part of the infant, this behavior was included in the behavioral pairings with both mother and infant behaviors. The high-risk day-care mothers were found both to talk and to touch more while they interacted with their infants without toys (IntW/OTalk $F_{1,57}$ = 5.828, p < .019 and IntW/OTouch $F_{1,57}$ = 5.603, p < .021).

Thus, these analyses indicate that the GPS and HRE samples perform quite similarly. It does appear that the GPS mothers, however, do make more attempts to capture the infants attention while he is playing alone by talking to him and by attempting to demonstrate toys to him. Nevertheless, these attempts do not appear to alter the frequency of the child's behavior.

The comparison of the HRE and the HRC groups seems to show that the HRE mothers, similar to the GPS mothers, had more difficulty in attracting the infant's attention by demonstrating toys. Further, the experimental group mothers appear more involved with their infants compared to the control group as indexed by more infant vocalizations when interacting with their mothers without toys. Finally, when the HRE mothers did interact without toys they both talked to and touched their infants more frequently.

Correlational Analysis of Mother-Infant Interaction Data

Intercorrelations between mother and infant behaviors over all groups presented in Table 3.9, revealed several strong relationships between the mother and infant behavior. Mothers who held their infants more spent more time on the furniture with the infants (Ω = .66, p < .001); had infants who were feeding or sleeping more

Table 3.9. Intercorrelations between Infant Variables Pearson Correlation Coefficients

Variables	Feed/sleep	Voc	Crib	Playtoys	Interact	Furn
Vocalization	-.34*					
In crib	.53***	-.20				
Play w toys	-.49***	.26*	-.32*			
Interact	-.09	-.14	-.09	-.56***		
Furniture	.27*	-.28*	.13	-.44***	.16	
Fuss/cry	.20	-.25	.32*	-.32*	-.17	.04

*p < .05
**p < .01 (none in this range)
***p < .001

(r = .49, p < .001) and who vocalized and played by themselves less (r = -.29, p < .05 and r = -.63, p < .001, respectively).

Mothers who talked more had infants who vocalized more (Ω = .27, p < .05). The infants also played less by themselves and interacted more with mother and toys (r = -.32, p < .01 and r = .49, p < .001, respectively).

The mothers interacting with their infants without the use of toys had infants who vocalized more (r = .46, p < .001) and played less by themselves (r = -.37, p < .01). Mothers who demonstrated toys had infants who vocalized less (r = -.26, p < .05), played less by themselves (r = -.54, p < .001), and interacted with the mothers with toys more (r = .90, p < .001).

Mothers who read to themselves had infants who played more by themselves and less with the mother with toys (r = .43, p < .001 and r = -.32, p < .05, respectively). The television being on appeared to vary only in relation to the infants interacting less with mother and toys (r = -.34, p < .01). The maternal behavior of reading to the child seemed to have no relation to infant behavior.

Home Observation for Measurement of the Environment

Mean comparisons on the six factors of the HOME across three groups involved using a multivariate analysis of variance. Scores on each of the six factors were analyzed to determine the differences among groups. The multivariate F test showed a significant difference (F mult.$_{12,104}$ = 7.486, p < .001), as did the univariate F tests of each factor (p < .001). The results of this analysis are presented in Table 3.10.

HRC vs. GPS. Special contrasts entailed comparing the high-risk control group with the general-population sample. Differences between the two groups were the same as between all three; each of the six factors were significant at the .001 level, with the GPS scoring higher.

HRE vs. HRC. Comparison between the two high-risk groups demonstrated no significant differences. The only factor to ap-

Table 3.10. Home Observation for Measurement of the Environment MANOVA

Multivariate F Test				
Test of Roots	F	DFHYP	DFERR	p
1 through 2	7.486	12.000	104.000	0.001
2 through 2	1.609	5.000	52.500	0.174
Univariate F Tests				
Variable	F(2,57)	MS	p	
Maternal warmth	12.122	27.432	0.001	
Absence of punishment	8.996	8.275	0.001	
Org of environment	14.576	10.817	0.001	
Appropriate toys	31.948	90.425	0.001	
Maternal involvement	28.755	48.900	0.001	
Opportunity for var	12.163	14.767	0.001	

proach significance was that of maternal involvement ($p < .055$), with the day-care group scoring *higher*.

Maternal Attitude Measures

The attitudinal measures were analyzed, using a multivariate analysis of variance.* The results of the three group comparison showed an overall difference significant at the .001 level. Univariate F tests demonstrated differences significant at the .001 level for the Rotter I-E Scale and the Authoritarian Control and Democratic Attitudes subscales of the PARI. The Hostility-Rejection subscale of the PARI was significant at the .027 level. Table 3.11 presents the results of this analysis.

HRC vs. GPS. When comparing the high-risk control groups with the general population sample, significant differences were identified on the Rotter and all three subscales of the PARI. The HRC scored higher on the Rotter I–E Scale, demonstrating a more external locus of control (HRC $\overline{X} = 11.933$, GPS $\overline{X} = 7.233$, $p < .001$). The HRC also scored higher on the Authoritarian Control subscale of the PARI (HRC $\overline{X} = 40.467$, GPS $\overline{X} = 23.833$, $p < .001$).

---

*Scoring on the PARI consisted of summing the items loading on the three subscales and adding a constant to eliminate negative sums.

Table 3.11. MANOVA for Rotter I-E and PARI Attitude Scales

Multivariate F Test

Test of Roots	F	DFHYP	DFERR	p
1 through 2	7.281	8.000	108.000	0.001
2 through 2	0.126	3.000	54.500	0.944

Univariate F Tests

SCALE	F (2,57)	MS	p
Rotter I-E	14.006	137.674	0.001
Authoritarian control	18.386	1710.146	0.001
Hostility-rejection	3.852	230.849	0.027
Democratic attitudes	28.251	1176.302	0.001

The GPS scored higher on the Hostility-Rejection and Democratic Attitudes subscales. On Hostility-Rejection, the GPS had a mean score of 57.433 and the HRC had a mean score of 50.993 (p < .010). The GPS Democratic Attitudes' mean score was 70.467 and the HRC's was 56.267 (p < .001).

HRE vs. HRC. Contrasts between the high-risk experimental and high-risk control groups demonstrated no significant differences between the two on either the Rotter I-E Scale or the three subscales of the PARI. Thus, the attitudes of these two groups do not appear to differ.

Relationship between Attitudes and Behavior

Attitudes and interaction data. In order to test the relationship between attitudes and behavior, correlation matrices were computed. Table 3.12 presents the Pearson product-moment correlation coefficients between the maternal attitude measures (Rotter I-E Scale and the PARI subscales) and the interaction variables that were significant at p < .05 level.

The results of the correlational analyses indicated that mothers who talked more had lower scores on the Rotter, demonstrating a more internal locus of control (r = −.31, p < .015), had lower scores on Authoritarian Control (r = −.38, p < .003) and higher scores on Democratic Attitudes (r = .33, p < .001).

Table 3.12 Relationship between Attitudes and Interaction Data

	Rotter I–E	Authoritarian control	Democratic attitudes
Talk to child	–.31*	–.38**	.33**
Furniture		.28*	
Read to child		–.26*	

*p < .05
**p < .01

Mothers scoring higher on the Authoritarian Control subscale of the PARI spent more time on the furniture with their infants (r = .28, p < .028), yet read to the infants less often (r = –.26, p < .044).

Attitudes and vocalization data. Specific correlation matrices were computed to determine the relationship between maternal attitudes and vocalization data which appeared particularly to differentiate the groups. Neither mother nor infant vocalizing in ten second blocks showed a positive relationship with higher Rotter and Authoritarian Control scores (r = .40, p < .002 and r = .44, p < .001, respectively) and a negative relationship with Democratic Attitudes (r = –.32, p < .012).

Mother vocalizing alone was positively associated with Democratic Attitudes (r = .38, p < .003) and negatively associated with Authoritarian Control (r = –.39, p < .002). Both mother and infant vocalizing together was negatively correlated with the Rotter I–E Scale (r = –.28, p < .033).

Table 3.13 presents these results.

HOME and interaction data. Correlation matrices were computed to determine the association between the interaction and attitudes measured in the home environment (HOME) and interaction measured in a controlled naturalistic setting. Results of this analysis showed a relationship between several of the variables in each measure. Table 3.14 presents the results of the correlations significant at p < .05 level.

Mothers achieving higher totals on the HOME talked to their infants more (r = .48, p < .001), but touched and turned the television on less (r = –.26, p < .047 and r = –.31, p < .014, re-

104   *Social Development in Childhood*

Table 3.13. Relationship between Attitudes and Vocalization Pearson Correlation Coefficients

	Rotter I–E	Authoritarian control	Hostility-rejection	Democratic attitudes
No Voc	.40**	.44***	.15	–.32**
Infant Voc	–.09	.10	–.03	–.20
Mother Voc	–.22	–.39**	.14	.38**
Both Voc	–.28	–.24	.08	.15

*p < .05 (none in this range)
*p < .01
***p < .001

spectively). Mothers scoring higher on the organization of the physical and temporal environment factor read to their infants more ($r = .30$, $p < .019$) and had the television on less ($r = -.32$, $p < .012$).

Mothers providing more appropriate toys for their infants spent less time on the furniture and had the television on less ($r = -.37$, $p < .004$ and $r = -.27$, $p < .038$, respectively). These same mothers talked to their infants more ($r = .36$, $p < .004$).

Mothers more involved with their infants, according to their scores on the HOME, talked to their infants more ($r = .56$,

Table 3.14. Relationship between HOME and Interaction Data Pearson Correlation Coefficients

	Total HOME	Org of environ	Approp toys	Maternal involvemt	Oppty for variety
In crib					.26*
On furn			–.37**		
Interact w M & toys				.34**	
Demonstrate				.30*	
Talk	.48***		.36**	.56***	.27*
TV on	–.31*	–.32*	–.27*	–.38**	–.37**
Read child		.30*		.28*	.28*
Read self				–.36**	–.36**
Touch	–.26*				

*p < .05
**p < .01
***p < .001

$p < .001$), demonstrated more toys ($r = .34$, $p < .008$), read to the infants more ($r = .28$, $p < .033$) and had infants who interacted with them with toys more ($r = .34$, $p < .008$). These mothers also spent less time with the television on and reading to themselves ($r = .38$, $p < .003$ and $r = -.36$, $p < .005$, respectively).

The mothers providing a greater opportunity for variety talked to their infants more ($r = .27$, $p < .035$), put the infants in the crib more ($r = .26$, $p < .041$) and turned on the television less ($r = -.37$, $p < .004$).

The factors of maternal warmth and the absence of punishment and hostility were not strongly associated with any of the interaction behaviors ($p > .05$).

Summary

Based upon the findings of the present investigation, significant differences were found in many areas of behavior. The high-risk infants receiving day-care and the general population sample were found to score significantly higher on the psychomotor index of the Bayley Developmental Scale than the high-risk home-reared infants. The high-risk day-care infants were found to more closely resemble the more advantaged infants in the general population than to resemble their control home-reared group.

On measures of mother-infant interaction patterns, significant variations were found among groups. Although there were not substantial differences in basic amounts of maternal care-taking behaviors (touching, holding, infant feeding/sleeping), infants playing alone or fussing/crying, mothers demonstrating toys or reading to themselves, differences were found in certain contrasts involving vocalization and interactive behaviors.

The high-risk group receiving day care was found to more closely approximate the general population sample than the high-risk home-reared group in the area of infant vocalization. High-risk infants in day care were found to vocalize at the same time as their mothers with similar frequency as the general population infants. High-risk infants being reared at home had less vocalization occurring in the same time interval as their mothers.

The high-risk day-care group was also found to interact more with their mothers both with and without toys. The HRE group responded more to their mothers' demonstration of toys and vocalized more when their mothers interacted with them without toys.

The general population sample scored higher on the HOME than either high-risk group. The two high-risk groups were found to have deprived homes, according to assessment by the HOME. The one factor indicating marginally significant differences between the high-risk samples was that of maternal concern for the development of the infant (maternal involvement) with the center-attending children receiving higher scores.

Maternal attitude measures were found to differentiate high-risk versus general samples. The mothers representing the high-risk groups were found to have a more perceived external locus of control, to be more authoritarian, less hostile and rejecting and less democratic.

On the relationship between attitudes and behavior, most associations were found in the vocalization behavior. Maternal vocalization was found to differentiate between authoritarian versus nonauthoritarian and democratic versus nondemocratic mothers. Alos, mothers talking more were found to have a more perceived internal locus of control.

Factors on the HOME were also found to be related to vocalization data. Mothers and infants vocalizing less were found to achieve lower scores on the HOME. Both mother and infant vocalizing together was found to be related to higher HOME scores, more maternal involvement, and more age-appropriate toys.

CONCLUSIONS

Being in a high-quality day-care program has apparently had a beneficial effect on the developmental status of high-risk infants. The high-risk infants enrolled in the Carolina Abecedarian Project were found to score significantly higher on the Bayley PDI than were their matched control infants being reared at home. The high-risk infants in day-care were found to have Bayley scores similar to the more advantaged infants being reared in the general population.

In addition to the improved developmental status, high-risk infants in day-care were found to have a social relationship with their mothers similar to that of the general population infants. Apparently there is not a negative relationship between being enrolled in a day-care program during the first year of life and having a high quality of interaction with the mother. The data would lead us to conclude that the Carolina Abecedarian Project has had a positive effect on the relationship between mother and infant.

The dissimilarity between the two high-risk groups seemed to reflect basic differences in the infants, rather than in the mothers. Also, vocalization appeared to be a particularly sensitive behavior differentiating among groups. The high-risk infants in day care were found to vocalize with similar frequency to the general population infants. While there were no significant differences between the two high-risk groups in the frequency count of mother vocalizing alone, there were significant differences in the frequency count of mother and infant vocalizing during the same time interval. Regardless of the direction of reinforcement (whether the mothers' vocalization reinforced the infants' vocalization or vice versa), there was a significant difference between the day-care and home-control high-risk groups on the measure of mother and infant vocalizing together.

Also, the finding that high-risk day-care infants interacted more with their mothers, while the mothers were demonstrating toys indicates a higher degree of responsivity on the part of these day-care infants. The high-risk day-care infants were found to respond with a greater frequency than were either the general population or high-risk home-reared infants.

Even though the high-risk mothers with infants enrolled in day-care behaved differently toward their infants during the observation taping in the controlled setting, there was limited generality to the home setting. Few differences were found when comparing the interaction between high-risk mothers and infants in their own homes. The one area in which differences were identified was that of maternal concern for optimal child development (HOME maternal involvement factor). The mothers with high-risk infants enrolled in day-care appeared more interested in the infants' development.

They reflected greater concern for providing a setting which would stimulate developmental advance.

Attitudes and behavior were related basically in the category of vocalization. Concurrent mother and infant vocalization appeared to be a good indicator of maternal locus of control and attitudes toward child-rearing. Mother and infant vocalizing together also appeared to indicate whether or not the home environment would be considered to be nondepriving, according to the Home Observation for Measurement of the Environment (HOME).

Impact in Day-Care Intervention

It seems reasonable to say, on the basis of findings in the present study, that within the first year of life positive effects seem to accrue for high-risk infants enrolled in the Carolina Abecedarian day-care program. Subsequent follow-up investigations will be needed to determine if the apparently beneficial effects evident in the first year of life continue.

The day-care program, as conceptualized and conducted at Frank Porter Graham Child Development Center in Chapel Hill, North Carolina, apparently is not detrimental to the social relationship between mother and infant. The program appears to have had no harmful effects on either the infant himself or on the infant's social relationship with his mother. If anything, the data suggests positive effects have accrued.

Day-care programs vary as to their quality, as do homes, and the extent to which these findings generalize to other day-care programs will require replication. Additional studies will be needed to determine whether or not other day-care programs are encouraging the infant and the infant's social relationship with his mother.

REFERENCES

Ainsworth, M. D. S. 1969. Object relations, dependency, and attachment: A theoretical review of the infant-mother relationship. *Child Development* 40: 969–1026.

Blehar, M. C. Anxious attachment and defensive reactions associated with day care (this volume).

Caldwell, B. M., Heider, J., & Kaplan, B. 1968. The inventory of home stimulation. Unpublished manuscript. Syracuse University.

Caldwell, B. M., Wright, C. M., Honig, A. S., & Tannenbaum, J. 1970. Infant care and attachment. *American Journal of Orthopsychiatry* 403: 397–412.

Deutsch, M., & Brown, B. 1964. Social influence on negro-white intelligence differences. *Journal of Social Issues* (April): 24–35.

Emmerich, W. 1969. The parental role: A functional-cognitive approach. *Society for Research in Child Development Monograph* 34, no. 8.

Golden, M., & Birns, B. 1971. Social class, intelligence, and cognitive style in infancy. *Child Development* 42: 2114–16.

Gordon, I. J. 1969. Early child stimulation through parent education. Final report to the Children's Bureau, Social and Rehabilitation Service, Department of Health, Education, and Welfare. PHS-R-306 (01) June 1969.

Gutelius, M. F., Kirsch, A. D., MacDonald, S., Brooks, M. R., McErlean, T., & Newcomb, C. 1972. Promising results from a cognitive stimulation program in infancy. *Clinical Pediatrics* 11: 585–93.

Heber, R. 1971. Rehabilitation of families at risk for mental retardation: A progress report. Madison, Wisconsin: University of Wisconsin (Rehabilitation Research and Training Center in Mental Retardation), October 1971.

Hunt, J. McV. 1961. *Intelligence and experience.* New York: Ronald Press Company.

Karnes, M. B., Teska, J. A., Hodgins, A. S., & Badger, E. D. 1970. Educational intervention at home by mothers of disadvantaged infants. *Child Development* 41: 925–36.

Klaus, R. A., & Gray, S. W. 1968. The early training project for disadvantaged children: A report after five years. *Monographs of the Society for Research in Child Development*, No. 120.

Levenstein, P. 1970. Cognitive growth in preschoolers through verbal interaction with mothers. *American Journal of Orthopsychiatry* 40 (3): 426–32.

Lewis, M., & Goldberg, S. 1969. Perceptual-cognitive development in infancy: A generalized expectancy model as a function of the mother-infant interaction. *Merrill-Palmer Quarterly* 15: 82–100.

Meier, J. 1972. *Screening and assessment of young children at developmental risk.* Denver: University of Colorado Medical Center.

Meier, J. H., Segner, L. L., & Grueter, B. B. 1970. An education system for high risk infants: A preventive approach to developmental and learning disabilities. In J. Hellmuth (ed.), *The disadvantaged child*, vol. III. New York: Brunner & Mazel.

Rotter, J. B. 1966. Generalized expectancies for internal vs. external control of reinforcement. Psychological Monographs: General and Applied 80 (1): 1–28.

Schaefer, E. S., & Bell, R. Q. 1958. Development of a parental attitude research instrument. *Child Development* 29: 339–61.

Social Research Group. 1971. A review of the present status and future needs in day care research. Washington, D.C.: George Washington University.

Stearns, M. S., Search, E. O., & Rosenfeld, A. H. 1971. Toward inter-agency coordination: An overview of federal research and development activities relating to early childhood, and recommendations for the future. A Report by the Interagency Panel on Early Childhood Research and Development, October 1971.

Stedman, D., Anastasian, N. J., Dokecki, P. R., Gordon, I. J., Parker, R. K. 1972. Study of educational intervention programs for children at risk of mental retardation. Report to the Department of Health, Education, and Welfare. HEW-OS-72-205.

4

THE SOCIALIZATION OF INTELLIGENCE: IMPLICATIONS FOR EDUCATIONAL INTERVENTION

Roger A. Webb, Mary Ellen Oliveri, and Frances S. Harnick

Psychologists have a way of returning to a nature-nurture controversy despite many demonstrations of the inherent weakness of such a simple, bivariate, distinction (Beach 1961; Lehrmann 1961; Hunt 1961; Piaget 1971). The recurrence of this interest is not difficult to understand—the contributions of hereditary and environmental factors to the development of both men and animals is is one of the abiding questions that have ramifications far beyond the narrow boundaries of academic discipline. What we have learned about the hereditary-environment distinction, however, is that once one has associated a particular behavior with either primarily hereditary or environmental factors, the task of understanding its development has only begun. Even taking a relatively straightforward example, such as sexual morphology, we find that the pathways from genetic information to manifestation in flesh and blood are complex and only partially understood (Money & Ehrhardt 1972). Thus, for students of development, detecting a relationship between some sets of events and a behavioral outcome is only a beginning. The real problem for developmental psychologists is to discover what processes mediate between genetic or environmental factors and their related behavioral outcomes.

The particular problem to which we address ourselves here is the study of the processes which mediate between social events and intellectual competence. One can reasonably assume—as these writers do—that basic structures of intelligence develop in what Piaget (1971) has called an "auto-regulated" fashion, with only minimal influence from variations in environments. One can further assume that a great deal of interindividual variance in intellectual efficiency, or power, can be attributed to hereditary factors. Despite both assumptions, however, one can still argue that intellectual competence in the final analysis depends to a great extent on the social milieu in which a child develops. Thus we entitle our chapter the "socialization of intelligence," to stress our belief that underlying operations of intelligence that may be best considered biological in nature take on their final form only when articulated in a social world.

To an investigator with a practical orientation, the social factors in intellectual growth (e.g., class experience, quality of the early home environment) are important not only because they appear to account for much of the interindividual and intergroup variance we see, but also because socially determined patterns of behavior are presumably open to intervention. Unfortunately, however, such general and amorphous terms as "social-class experience" are difficult to investigate and the the realities to which they refer are even more difficult to change. As we have suggested above, the most interesting and potentially profitable questions for research must be concerned with *how* certain social and environmental circumstances produce certain intellectual consequences.

At first glance, there appear to be at least three distinct, although interrelated, processes by which social factors mediate intellectual growth. First, a secure attachment with a mother or mother figure appears to facilitate exploration and play in infancy (Ainsworth & Bell 1969; Harlow & Harlow 1969; Main 1973; Rheingold & Eckerman 1969), and these activities seem to be essential aspects of intellectual growth. Main (1973), in fact, has demonstrated not only that a secure attachment relationship can mediate intellectual performance by modifying play, exploration, and social interaction but also that securely attached children outperformed insecurely attached children by about 15 points on the Bayley Mental Scale. Main argued that the gain in DQ points was due, in part, to the social skill shown by the secure children in dealing with the examiner.

A second role that social factors play in intellectual growth is the providing of models for incorporation into the child's behavioral repertoire. Due perhaps to the pervasive influence of Piagetian constructivist epistemology, the role of models in the development of intelligence has been a relatively neglected topic in recent years— with the notable exception of the work of Jerome Bruner (1971). Most of the work on modeling (e.g., Bandura 1969) has been concerned with socialization per se (e.g., why some models are accepted more readily than others; Flanders 1968) rather than with the incorporation of intellectual skills. It is possible to assert, however, that modeling processes are essential to the child's intellectual growth. In infancy, social models may demonstrate patterns of reciprocal play which may, in turn, constitute prototypes for later instructional interactions. In later childhood, children are expected to incorporate many specific models of both behavioral skills (e.g., how to ride a bicycle) and intellectual skills (e.g., mathematical operations of algebra). Neither of these abilities follows automatically from the self-regulated intellectual development of the child, but depends on the incorporation of cultural tools. While there are certainly constraints—both motoric and intellectual—that limit the process of acculturation, competence is as much a function of the tools available in one's culture and the use one puts them to as of any intrinsic factor.

The third role that social factors play in intellectual growth, and the primary topic for discussion here, is the socialization of a child to the intellectual world view of his social group; this topic appears to have considerable relevance for ethnic and social-class differences in intellectual performance, and for the problem of educational intervention. If it may be assumed that a child's "intellectual" approach to life is shaped by the availability of cultural models and the quality (e.g., security or insecurity) of his relationship with significant persons, the question still remains: to what is the child being socialized? How does his social experience affect his approach to intellectual activity? The thesis of this paper is that there are important and pervasive differences in the intellectual functioning of children that may not be tapped by conventional IQ and achievement measures and that are closely related to particular kinds of social experience.

Returning to our original point, we can see from Hess's (1970) review that there is a major controversy over the means by which ethnic and social class factors affect the development of children. Often the effects themselves are well-known—as in the connection between social class and school performance, or between race and IQ in this country—but there is essentially no understanding of what processes mediate the relationship. Social class may—to follow the line of Jensen (1969) or Herrnstein (1973)—represent society's sorting itself out on the basis of innate intelligence. Still, work by Hess and others (Bernstein 1970; Hess & Shipman 1965; Bee, et al. 1969; Greenfield & Bruner 1969) suggest that the way in which children are socialized may have an important influence on the way they think, affecting their intelligence in the broad sense.

But what do we mean by "intelligence in the broad sense"? We would like to propose that to examine the effects of social experience on children's intellectual performance in a sufficiently complex fashion, we must attempt to escape the rubrics within which intelligence is conventionally viewed. We have argued elsewhere (see Webb, Oliveri, & Harnick 1974) that the two major approaches to intelligence—Piagetian and psychometric—may each be inadequate both for assessing the effects of socializing practices on intelligence and for providing a framework for the institution and evaluation of compensatory educational intervention. The "structures" of human intelligence, in the Piagetian sense, are universal or, perhaps, species-specific behaviors that are seen to develop in similar fashion in all children; as such, they should not be particularly appropriate for, or susceptible to, modification by any less than extreme environmental variation. On this point we are in essential agreement with Ginsburg (1972), who contends that there are few critical differences in intellectual development between the so-called "culturally deprived" child and the middle-class child. We disagree, however, that Ginsburg's analysis is complete and contend that class differences in other areas of intelligence are real and important.

A psychometric approach to educational intervention creates related problems in that intelligence as assessed through IQ tests appears to be one of the more stable of human characteristics after about the age of four (Bloom 1964), and to be determined to a great degree by hereditary factors (Vandenberg 1971). Even though it is quite possible to modify IQ scores in the short run through a variety of programs (e.g., see reviews by Bereiter 1972; Bronfenbrenner 1974; Karnes 1973) the long-range benefits of such intervention are still in doubt. It has been found—apparently without exception—that within one to two years after children leave intervention programs their tested IQ's decline to the levels of untreated controls (see reviews above). Most investigators imply that this so called "fade-out effect" is due to the child's return to his debilitating environment (Bereiter 1972; Weikert 1972) and there is at least one explicit model of the phenomenon (Campbell & Frey 1970). We would argue, on the other hand, that the fade-out effect is inherent in the nature of the IQ test, which by definition is a measure of the performance of a child relative to the average child of the same age. As children get older, the test content changes, and the skills that have been taught in the intervention program are no longer relevant to test performance. Psychometric IQ thus appears an unsuitable choice as the standard of success in educational intervention.

The approach that appears more appropriate and of more potential long-range benefit is concentration upon what we have termed *style* (Webb et al. 1974). Two or more individuals with identical intellectual structures and similar IQ's may still respond in different ways when faced with a problem demanding intellectual activity. In that their mode of responding is a relatively consistent aspect of their intellectual performance, it may be considered their style. Important aspects of style appear, in turn, to be determined to a great extent by social events.

The postulation of a dimension of intellectual style that is determined in large part by social experience receives support in the literature from Bernstein's (1970) notion of restricted and elaborated communication codes, Sigel's (Sigel, Secrist, & Forman 1973) notion of "distancing," and the increasing body of work on the verbal mediation of memory (e.g., see Flavell 1970). Bernstein (1970), for example, argues that particular forms of social-class experience shape particular modes of communication. The economic circumstances of the lower class are said to create a culture where "we" is emphasized over "I," and where many identifications, experiences, and assumptions are closely shared. In this type of social situation, there appears little need for detailed verbal explication of meanings, motives, or feelings; consequently, a "restricted code" arises which is composed of context-dependent utterances with implicit and particularistic (tied to the immediate situation) meanings. The social situation of the middle class, however, is said to emphasize "I" over "we"; the intent of other speakers cannot often be taken for granted, and speakers are encouraged to elaborate meanings and make them more explicit and specific. Thus, middle-class speakers are seen to develop the tendency toward an "elaborated code," which embodies more context-independent utterances whose meanings are explicit and universalistic (transcending the immediate situation). The elaborated-restricted code distinction also implies a second important feature of intellectual style. The degree to which a child believes the world is amenable to rational understanding and that his own efforts are effective in modifying it will vary as a function of culture (Greenfield & Bruner 1969) and of social group (Bernstein 1970).

Although Bernstein emphasizes that a restricted code should not be devalued as a mode of communication within a particular social context, it does not appear adaptive in a school context where communication of explicit, abstract, and universalistic meanings is expected. "Thus between the school and the community of the working-class child there may exist a cultural discontinuity based upon two radically different systems of communication" (Bernstein 1970, p. 29). This is, then, one dimension of what we are calling "style"—the tendency (or lack thereof) to communicate interindividually in an explicit, abstract, and meaningful manner, with understanding and anticipation of the perspective of one's partner (see Garvey & Hogan 1973, for a sample of young children's competence in these matters).

The notion of style can also embody, however, the adaptive use of intraindividual communication, that is, the characteristic use of one's representational abilities of memory and language to "help oneself" intellectually (see Carroll 1964). This is what is implied in Sigel's "distancing hypothesis,'—the notion that not all children automatically *use* their representational abilities to their best advantage when confronted with tasks demanding intellectual activity. Sigel advocates teaching children to do so by stressing the abstract and the nonpresent as opposed to only the concrete and the present; the point is to encourage children to use their representational skills to create some distance between themselves and the immediate situation—to make themselves "step back," as it were, and give themselves a chance to think and talk about what they are doing and perceiving.

Style should be considered an intellectual *Weltanschuung*, a characteristic way of approaching intellectual tasks in general that may be reflected in a number of specific behavioral strategies. Keeney, Cannizzo, and Flavell (1967), for example, showed that first-graders who spontaneously used verbal mediation in a memory task performed better than those who did not, but that the performance of nonmediators improved upon the simple instruction to verbalize. Use of verbal mediation thus appears to be a highly effective intraindividual strategy. The failure to mediate, however, may be part of a more general failure to use language and other representational skills in an adaptive manner (Bruner 1971), and thus might well be related to social-class experience. At the present time, it can only be surmised that distinct social-class differences exist in the use of intraindividual representational strategies, such as verbal mediation; a study currently underway, however (see below), is, in part, an attempt to identify any such differences.

To the extent that one's intellectual style—both inter- and intraindividual—is determined by social experience, it should be open to remedial influences—at least with very young children. To the extent that it is effectively modified, the benefits to later school-related activity may be substantial, if the modification is strong enough to withstand the vicissitudes of everyday life. For, as Bernstein (1970) and Hess (1970) imply, what might be considered a maladaptive style in dealing with intellectual tasks arises as an *adaptive* response to a pervasive and persistent social context. Unless that social context changes, certain stylistic predispositions arising from and reinforced by that context may be highly resistant to long-term modification, a possibility of which optimistic and well-intentioned investigators should be aware.

In our attempt to study the nature of style and its implications for educational intervention, we have been led to three types of study. The first is an experimental intervention effort within Baltimore City nursery schools. This study is an attempt to modify the communicative interaction styles of the teachers when dealing with children and an assessment of the program's effect on the children's intellectual performance. The second study is a similar experimental effort within the newly founded Baltimore Infant/Parent Center for Education. The third is a shorter-range attempt both to identify social-class differences in the effective use of intraindividual language strategies in specific preschool tasks, and to assess the immediate effectiveness of a modification of those strategies. These three experimental efforts are aimed at the modification of various aspects of the general notion of style, and will be discussed in turn below.

1. The Preschool Curriculum Study

In September 1972, the present writers undertook to transmit a "style-oriented" cognitive curriculum to the teachers and children in a series of Baltimore City nursery schools (see Webb et al. 1974, for further details on the curriculum and evaluation). Sixteen schools, which were already part of an ongoing nursery school program for a lower-income, predominantly black group of children, were randomly assigned to experimental and control groups. We attempted no instructional interaction with the teachers in the control schools. We did, however, meet with them occasionally over the course of the study to tell them that they were a vital part of an experiment and to explain the testing procedures that would be used. Otherwise, control teachers continued with their classroom activities as they had before. To the experimental teachers, we provided a supplement that consisted primarily of a series of nine lesson plans that were distributed and discussed at biweekly teacher meetings.

The specific method of teacher-training employed deserves comment. Based upon evidence that *deductive* teacher-training methods are difficult to implement and that detailed, highly structured programs are implemented quickly and thoroughly (Bissell 1973; Haith 1972), the present writers opted for the latter, *inductive*, approach. So, instead of giving the teachers abstract, theoretical training and expecting the teachers to translate general theoretical notions into appropriate classroom activity, we gave the teachers in our study very detailed and specific instructions for classroom activity in the form of the lesson plans. Although the teachers were informed, midway through the training year, of the general goals of our curriculum and were encouraged to extend the type of interaction exemplified by the lesson plans to all of their activities with the children, the lesson plans provided a simple and quick means of initially implementing the curriculum.

Each lesson plan had two levels of content. The first was specific to individual lessons (for example, instructions for how to tell a story or a pouring exercise dealing with the concept of volume). The second level of content, however, was implicit in *all* of the lessons and consisted of the type of teacher-child interaction that the curriculum was designed to foster. This type of interaction embodied Sigel's notion of "distancing" and Bernstein's emphasis upon the school-related importance of elaborated modes of communication. The teachers were encouraged, by means of the lesson plans, to talk to the children in elaborated codes, and to lead the children to try to comprehend the events in their lives in more abstract terms and use their representational skills to escape the bounds of the immediate situation.

So, for example, the children were called upon to remember and anticipate a sequence of actions involved in making play-dough, or in setting a table for juice- or meal-time, or in the telling of a story. In all of the lessons, the children were encouraged to think about *nonpresent* objects, people, or situations, that is, those separated from the child by distance, time, or opportunity. Thinking about casual contingencies was also stressed; for example, a teacher's saying, "What will happen if I do this?" and, "Well, what would have happened if I had done something else?" Finally, in all of the lesson-plan activities, children were specifically encouraged to put their activities, thoughts, and feelings into words. In short, the children were given the opportunity and encouragement for thinking about what they did and saw happening around them, for talking about it, and, hopefully, for coming to some realization that communication and interaction with the people and things around them can make for an enjoyable and profitable learning situation.

In assessing the effectiveness of our curriculum after the first year, we undertook two separate types of evaluation. First, in order to determine whether and how well the curriculum was actually transmitted, we made time-sampled observations of the classroom behavior of both the experimental and control teachers. Three observers who were naive both to the aims of the curriculum and to the status (experimental or control) of the schools were trained on a 17-category checklist adapted from Sigel et al. (1972). In an experimental school, codings were made both on a lesson-plan activity and on a non-lesson-plan directed activity. In a control school, codings were made on two separate directed activities.

The pattern of intercorrelations among the 17 coded categories revealed that the data could be collapsed into seven categories for analysis. These were: (1) Questions: the total number of questions asked; (2) Brief responses: the number of questions requiring only a one-word answer or a motor response; (3) Descriptions: the number of statements in which the teacher utilized description or explanation; (4) Complex processes: The number of times the teacher utilized transformation, classification, pantomime, anticipation, recollection, and elaboration; (5) Classroom directions: the number of directives, corrections, and validations; (6) Noninformation: the number of other codings; and (7) Lack of verbal output: the number of intervals in which the teacher did not verbalize.

Analysis of the teacher-observation data using multivariate analysis of variance revealed a significant difference between experimental lesson-plan activity and control-directed activity (multivariate $F (7,8) = 3.98$, $p < .04$), with the complex processes category contributing most to the group differences. The experimental teachers were significantly higher than the controls in use of complex processes behavior ($F (1,14) = 35.84$, $p. < .001$); they were also significantly lower than the controls in use of noninformation behavior ($F (1,14) = 4.60$, $p < .05$).

Additional analyses revealed, however, that the particular type of classroom activity generated by the lesson plans did not generalize outside of specific lesson-plan activities. Significant differences were found in complex processes codings between experimental lesson plan activity and experimental nonlesson plan directed activity (F $(1,14) = 9.00$, p $< .01$). Also, no differences were found between experimental nonlesson plan directed activity and control directed activity. The results indicated, then, that the lesson plan strategy was effective in changing the experimental teachers' behavior in the desired direction during the structured portions of the curriculum. That this modification did not generalize outside of specific lesson plan activity is unfortunate, but could be due in part to the relatively brief period of time the program had been operative up to the time of the first-year evaluation.

Three incidental facts emerging from correlational analyses of the complex process data should be cited. Because of the small n's (eight for each) the correlations are not statistically significant; they are, however, relatively high, replicate findings in the literature, and appear worth reporting. Complex processes behavior correlated positively with previously obtained supervisor's ratings of teacher quality in the experimental group ($r = +.45$), and negatively in the control group ($r = -.51$). This may indicate that the "better teacher" is the one who is most able to apply what she has learned when training is provided, but that the complex processes behavior was not part of the definition of good teaching in this particular program prior to our intervention. Additional correlational analyses compared complex processes behavior with the educational level of the teachers. For the experimental teachers, the correlation was positive but low ($r = .15$); for the controls, however, the correlation was higher ($r = .48$). These findings suggest that as long as both structure and supervision are supplied in a program the educational level of the teachers is relatively unimportant, but that better educated teachers generally use more complex processes. Finally, we are impressed by the overall low level of complex processes behavior in what we believe was a good nursery school program. Despite protestations of our teachers, they were not leading the children to an elaborated use of thought and language to any great extent before we intervened.

Our second task in assessing the value of our intervention was the evaluation of the program's effect on the children's intellectual performance. Accordingly, all available children between the ages of three years and four years, eight months at the end of the first year in each of the experimental and control schools were tested. The test battery was partially composed of the following items from the Stanford–Binet:

> Three-hole form board (form L–M, year II)
> Three-hole form board, rotated (form L–M, year II–6)
> Picture vocabulary (form L–M, year II)
> Identifying parts of the body (form L–M, year II)
> Comprehension I (form L–M, year III–6):
>   "What must you do when you're thirsty?"
>   "Why do we have stoves?"
> Block-building—Bridge (form L–M, year III): model present and absent

The remaining items in the battery were four classification tasks (identify matching and large/small classification), two examples of a modification of the Sigel Memory Matching Test (Sigel, Secrist, & Forman 1972) and a pantomime task adapted from Sigel et al. 1972).

Sixteen testers, naïve both to the goals of the experimental curriculum and to which schools were experimental and which control, were trained and organized into eight teams. Each team tested children in one experimental and one control school.

In addition to the test battery, a standardized rating of social competency was obtained for each of the children at the end of the school year using the California Preschool Social Competency Scale (Levine, Elzey, & Lewis 1969).

At the outset of the project certain predictions were made concerning the outcome of the test results. Since our curriculum aimed at modifying style rather than knowledge of specific content, it was anticipated that only the comprehension, memory matching, and pantomime items should show clear differences in favor of the experimental children. We were uncertain as to whether the classification items should show any differences, and we predicted that the remaining items in the test battery should show no differences between the experimental and control groups. In addition, because we had a certain amount of faith in the interdependency of cognitive and social skills, and because our cognitive input was transmitted by means of social interaction, it was anticipated that the experimental children would exceed controls on social competency ratings.

Preliminary unvariate analyses of variance performed on all test measures revealed that, although a ceiling was reached on a few of the easier items, the experimental children performed better than the controls on the majority of the test items, statistically significantly so on the identity matching, picture vocabulary, and comprehension items. The control children did not perform significantly better than the experimentals on any items.

A more revealing analysis resulted, however, when the entire group of children was split at the median age of three years, eight months, and the resulting age groups were analyzed separately. The results of this analysis provided a partial confirmation of our original predictions. The younger experimental children significantly outperformed the younger control children only on the picture vocabulary item (F (1,54) = 8.48, $p < .005$). The older experimental children, however, exceeded the older control children on one identity matching item (F (1,55) = 3.62, $p < .062$), the second comprehension question (F (1,55) = 2.86, $p < .096$), one memory matching item (F (1,55) = 3.62, $p < .062$), and pantomime (F (1,55) = 3.42, $p < .070$). A composite "distancing" measure, obtained by adding scores from the pantomime, memory matching, and comprehension items, also produced a difference in favor of the older experimental children (F (1,55) = 4.73, $p < .034$). Although the differences found between the groups of older children did not reach high levels of statistical significance, the pattern of differences is fairly clear. Our curriculum appeared to have differential effects depending upon the ages of the children tested. In children under three years, eight months, vocabulary skills were improved, while in children above that age, the behaviors that are seen as representative of "distancing," and practically only those measures showed differences approaching statistical significance.

The experimental children also signficantly exceeded the controls on total social competency scores (F (1,97) = 4.03, $p < .047$). Many of the specific items of the scale that showed significant group differences appeared to be cognitive items rather than purely social ones—for example, following instructions, explaining things to other children, adapting to changes in routine, and using the names of other children. We interpret the social competency results with some caution, however, since the social competency scores do derive from teachers' ratings, and, obviously, the teachers were aware of their role as participants in an experiment.

In conclusion, then, the results of the first-year evaluation of our preschool curriculum program suggest that an emphasis upon *style*, as defined herein, is amenable to incorporation into a structured curriculum, and that our curriculum was moderately successful in modifying aspects of behavior that, according to the theoretical analysis presented, might be predicted to change. Unfortunately, we can make no claims at present that a program such as this will resist the almost inevitable "fade-out" of effects that has plagued many experimental preschool programs. We feel justified in arguing, however, that striving through social means to change habits that appear to arise as a result of social circumstances is a quite practical and potentially useful enterprise that merits further concentrated attention from preschool educators.

2. The Baltimore Infant/Parent Center for Education

Our moderate degree of success with the preschool curriculum led us to investigate the utility of the notion of style in another context. If certain stylistic predispositions are environmentally determined, presumably the earlier one attempts to foster them, the better. Accordingly, we extended our study and our intervention efforts to infants. To understand how the notion of style relates to very young children, however, we must focus on slightly different aspects of intellectual performance than we discussed above. The concept of distancing that constituted much of the basis of our preschool curriculum is not applicable to infants in the sensorimotor period. Distancing refers to the use of representational abilities to escape the bounds of immediate experience—abilities that we assume do not appear until about the age of two. There are, however, behaviors within the infant's repertoire that may be critical features of his developing intellectual style. Reciprocal play and preverbal communication may be viewed as analogous to and forerunners of later linguistic communication, instructional interactions, and such basic social skills as turn-taking. It does not appear unreasonable, then, to speak of a style-oriented curriculum for infants.

In January of 1974, the Baltimore City school system opened the Infant/Parent Center for Education, which provided us the opportunity to investigate the utility of a style-oriented curriculum for infants. The center enrolled twenty black low-income mothers and their five- to twelve-month-old infants. The experimental school sample was randomly selected from a population of forty such mother-infant pairs; the remaining twenty were incorporated into a home-visit program in which a community worker visited the homes once a month. The experimental mother-infant pairs attended school three days a week, from 9:00 A.M. to 2:30 P.M., from January through June. One day a week, the paraprofessionals who worked with the babies in the school made home visits.

Programs were established for both mothers and infants. The mothers received vocational training as well as academic instruction in preparation for the high school equivalency examination. They also attended classes in parent education, during which proper activities for infants, child growth and development, and the "care and feeding" of the human infant were discussed. Mothers were responsible for feeding their own children and spent a half-hour each week observing the infant classrooms.

The infant program staff was composed of ten paraprofessionals and a teacher. Two infants were assigned to each paraprofessional, with four infants in each room. Each baby was allowed to set his own pace for eating and sleeping but most fell into a set routine. In general, the goal of the school was to give the infants a wide range of perceptual and motor activities in a secure but challenging environment. In addition to this general plan, the cognitive curriculum developed by Frances Harnick was used at times during the day when the baby was awake and alert.

The curriculum was a developmentally based set of lesson plans. Activities were developed by compiling knowledge and research on infant behavior from five to twenty-four months of age and cataloguing it on a month-to-month basis. The lessons were devised so as to capitalize on the infant's current level of ability while directing and extending efforts toward future abilities.

The lesson plans were each organized on three conceptual levels. The first of these levels was content, which varied from plan to plan. Many of these lessons concerned the developing sensory and motor systems. Activities stressing prehension, eye-hand coordination, and balance would be of this type. Another area of content was related to perceptual discrimination and included figure/ground and stimulus differentiation activities. Piagetian-based lesson plans included object permanence games and activities using means/ends differentiation.

The second conceptual level of the lesson plans involved the particular methods used in carrying out an activity. The specific teaching strategies conveyed by the lessons were goal orientation, demonstration, imitation, and verbalization. These behaviors help untangle means from end, provide relevant social models, and promote adaptive styles of social interaction. For example, the lesson for the "pop-up" telephone involved showing the child the figure that jumped out, demonstrating and verbalizing how to make it pop up, and encouraging the child to imitate.

The third conceptual level was most complex and consisted of the style of interaction used while working with the infants. In our earlier curriculum work, we believe we demonstrated that the structured lesson plan approach can be extremely effective at producing even complex interaction patterns. The particular style inherent in these plans relied on two types of interaction; the first of these is referred to here as "spacing" and the second as "contingency." Spacing is the practice of leaving an interval of time after performing some action, particularly in the presence of another person. During this interval, the first person orients and attends to the reactions of the second, observing the results of his own action. For example, after showing the baby how to use the toy telephone, the paraprofessional stopped to watch what effect it had produced and also to give the baby a chance to respond.

Spacing has several beneficial effects. First, it moves the focus of attention from the execution of an act to its consequences. As far as this curriculum was concerned, spacing also allowed for a time during which the aide could assess the baby's feelings and reactions as a result of her own actions; by "tuning in" the aide to the baby in this manner, it was hoped that a more sensitive interaction would take place. Spacing should also be effective in producing turn-taking behavior, which is an extremely adaptive social strategy. In addition, it should help develop a positive self-concept, since the baby sees that his reactions are attended to and are important.

The other style of interaction fostered by the curriculum was contingency. Watson (1966, 1972) has related contingency experience to cognitive development in infancy. Watson proposes that an infant is presented the problem of figuring out the world and where he belongs in it. Because of this, the infant is determined to isolate all of the relevant components of a situation. If the situation is one in which cause/effect relations and contingencies are consistent, the infant can unravel the connections and is content; if, however, the observed events are not contingent on one another, and results are not consistent, then the baby experiences negative affect. It has been demonstrated elsewhere that if a mother is consistent in her behavior, with all responses contingent on the same stimuli, the infant is better adjusted; inconsistent mothering results in a confused and unhappy baby (Ainsworth 1973). Appreciation of contingency is, of course, at the heart of both social and behavioral theories of learning; it is a necessary correlate of imitation and operant learning.

Evaluations of the program after the first six months have been made and data are currently being analyzed. Experimental and control infants were pre- and posttested with the Mental Scale of the Bayley Infant Scales of Development. In addition, at the time of posttesting, all mother-infant pairs were observed in free-play situations. Home observations were made, using Caldwell's Family Data Inventory. While analyses of the data are far from complete, some tentative conclusions have emerged from the data.

While the Bayley scores of the experimental and control groups were nearly identical at the time of the pretest (mean DQ = 104.00 and 108.00, respectively), the posttest scores differed by about one standard deviation (experimental mean DQ = 117.08, control mean DQ = 100.67; $F (1,22) = 7.85$, $p < .01$). A look at the ceiling level reached on the pre- and posttests suggests a developmental arrest in the control group by the time of the second testing, while the experimental group is continuing to acquire new behaviors. We believe this shift represents changes in the behaviors assessed by the

Bayley over time. Items that contribute variance to early Bayley scores are by and large perceptual-motor items, and both groups of subjects were relatively precocious with respect to these behaviors at the time of the pretest. As subjects grow older, however, the items that differentiate the children become more cognitive-social-linguistic in nature; these behaviors do not seem to be developing well in the control group.

Information was also obtained from the Infant Behavior Record (IBR) which accompanies the Bayley Test. Experimental infants showed a significantly higher degree of object orientation (F (1,22) = 8.80, p < .007), goal directedness (F (1,22) = 8.29, p < .009), and longer attention span (F (1,22) = 4.33, p < .05). They were more interested in all sorts of sensory stimulation (F (1,22) = 7.83, p < .01), and showed better fine (F (1,22) = 6.49, p < 02) and gross (F (1,22) = 7.02, p < .02) motor coordination. Also, although the video recordings of the infant/mother play session have not yet been completely coded, it appears that the experimental infants show a greater interest in toys and are more content to explore on their own during solitary play. Yet, when it is time to interact with their mothers they do so with pleasure.

To date, the evidence from our evaluation of the Baltimore Infant/Parent Center for Education suggests results similar to those obtained by other investigators (Caldwell & Richmond 1969; Heber et al. 1972, as cited in Bronfenbrenner 1974; Keister 1970). Unfortunately, as in most of these studies, the primary evidence currently available is based upon a single measuring instrument—the Bayley Infant Scales. Further analysis of the data obtained from the infant school and follow-up testings are required to determine whether the differences between the groups may be considered evidence for a stylistic dimension of infant intelligence.

3. Social-Class Effects upon Intra-Individual Language Strategies

In the two studies just described, the approach taken toward understanding the social determinants of intellectual competence consisted of modifying the general communicative interaction styles of teachers and assessing the effects on the children through a set of related behavioral measures. As was noted above, however, we consider "style" to be a general approach toward intellectual activity that is determined by social experience and that may encompass various specific strategies. A study currently underway, conducted by Mary Ellen Oliveri, is an effort at understanding the ramifications of social-class experience for one particular stylistic strategy—the intraindividual use of language to mediate cognitive performance.

There is reason to believe (Bernstein 1970) that social-class experience can shape *inter*individual communication styles; in fact, Tough (1970) has provided evidence on the communicative language use of preschoolers that further substantiates Bernstein's view. The social-class determinants of such intraindividual communication strategies as verbal mediation, however, are as yet unclear. As was noted above, the present writers consider both inter- and intraindividual communication strategies to reflect the intellectual dimension of "style," and to be, quite possibly, interrelated and interdependent. Unfortunately, there have yet to be few, if any, systematic attempts to delineate their interrelationships. Types of research appear to fall into quite distinct groups: on the one hand are investigators with an individual and social-class-differences orientation toward studying language as a *social* tool (Bernstein 1960, 1962*a*, 1962*b*; Entwisle 1968; Entwisle & Greenberger 1969; Lawton 1964; Robinson 1965*a*, 1965*b*; Tough 1970); on the other, are the experimentally and normatively oriented researchers studying specific ways language can function as a cognitive tool, with little apparent interest in individual or social-class differences (Bush & Cohen 1970; Dale 1969; Flavell 1970; Kendler & Kendler 1962; Kingsley & Hagen 1969; Luria 1969; Vygotsky 1962; Weir & Stevenson 1959). Although Cazden (1966) has stressed the importance of studying if and how subcultural differences in the use of language for interindividual communication affects its use as an intraindividual cognitive tool, and Jensen (1968) and John and Goldstein (1964) have advocated investigation of social-class differences in language as a mediator of cognitive performance, little systematic investigation has yet been undertaken.

The current investigation is, in large part, an attempt to answer the following questions: Do lower-class children really use language (intraindividually as well as interindividually) differently from middle-class children? Does the intraindividual use of language by lower-class children impede their performance on school-related tasks? Are all of these phenomena products of socialization and not merely dependent upon IQ? Is the use of language when performing intellectual tasks modifiable and, if so, will the inducement of a potentially more adaptive intraindividual language strategy help to improve performance on school-related tasks?

At the time this paper is being written, data have been collected on the likelihood of spontaneous verbalization during performance of simple pictorial memory tasks in small samples of middle- and lower-class nursery school children. The data indicate so far that nearly 100 percent of the middle-class children spontaneously name the pictures they are to remember. Lower-class children appear to do so less; our estimates of the incidence of spontaneous verbalization among these children range from 45 percent to 80 percent, depending upon the situational context and the specific form of the task employed. In order to determine if this pattern of differences holds up on a large scale and with additional tasks, further study is under way.

Subjects are black middle-class, white middle-class, black lower-class, and white lower-class nursery school children. The following data are currently being collected on every child: (1) IQ as assessed by the Slosson Intelligence Test; (2) a measure of interindividual "communicative competence" aimed at assessing the context-independent and elaborated nature of a child's communicated description of a picture; (3) rate of spontaneous verbalization during task performance and adequancy of task performance on three otherwise nonverbal tasks: pictorial memory as assessed through a delayed matching-to-sample task, memory for colored block arrangements, and classification.

It is expected (based upon the evidence contributed by Bernstein 1960, 1970, and Tough 1970) that middle-income children will use language in a more context-independent and elaborated fashion than will the lower-class children in the interindividual "communicative competence" task. The major question in this phase of research, however, is whether middle-class children also exceed lower-class children in the incidence of intraindividual communication in the form of overt verbal mediation during cognitive task performance. If inter- and intraindividual communication styles are indeed reflections of the same socialization process, this should be the case; further, as there is ample evidence that verbal mediation can enhance performance on nonverbal tasks, a pattern of social-class differences in overt verbalization during task performance could constitute one explanation for any social-class differences in actual task performance found.

Our expectation with regard to the relationship of the phenomena being studied to IQ needs some comment. As stressed above, we do consider certain stylistic predispositions such as the use of inter- and intraindividual language strategies to result, in large part, from social-class experience; unfortunately, social-class membership and IQ are undoubtedly related. Accordingly, social-class differences in the IQ scores of the samples of children being tested might parallel (at least somewhat) the differences obtained in the measures under current consideration and could tend to cloud interpretation of the causal factors.

Thus, even after the data just described are in, IQ might still be a problem confusing interpretation. Also, the environmental lability of such an intra-individual strategy might still be somewhat unclear. The next step for study would appear to be to conduct an experimental modification of intraindividual language use with IQ controlled, and this is planned. The point of this next phase of study is to determine to what extent social-class differences in cognitive task performance can be overcome, in the short run, simply by inducing the presumably adaptive strategy of verbal mediation.

A subset of children from each of the four social-class/racial groups will be matched on IQ and previous rate of spontaneous verbalization, and will be randomly assigned to experimental and control groups. What is planned is to retest the children on modified forms of the cognitive tasks described above; the experimental treatment, however, will consist of explicit encouragement to the children to use language as a mediator when performing the tasks (i.e., naming pictures and blocks for memory, and labeling dimensions for classification).

The results of this experimental effort could provide one explanation for lower-class children's relatively poor performance on school-related tasks. If children who do not characteristically use language as a mediator in cognitive tasks can be encouraged to do so, and if the inducement of a presumably adaptive style of intraindividual language use can be a facilitating factor in performance of nonverbal tasks (regardless of IQ constraints), the experimental children in this phase of study should out-perform the controls on the cognitive tasks. Also, the magnitude of social-class differences in task performance should be smaller in the experimental than in the control group, indicating to what extent such an intervention can overcome effects of social-class experience.

At this point, we feel pangs of conscience for describing at some length the predicted outcome of a study that has only begun. We hope that the reader will realize, however, that this type of short-term study of one particular stylistic strategy is a necessary complement to the intervention studies described above, and thus justifies elaboration herein. In the intervention efforts, we modified the interindividual communicative interaction styles of teachers on the assumption that adaptive inter- and intraindividual communication styles would be induced in the children. What was assessed, however, was the children's performance on various measures that were presumed to reflect the cognitive outcome of the general dimension of "style." We obtained results that were supportive of this presumption, but the question still remains as to what particular stylistic strategies might be responsible. The current study is an attempt to clarify the picture somewhat by investigating the social-class-relatedness of one particular intraindividual strategy and examining to what extent the inducement of its use can overcome—at least in the short run—social-class constraints on cognitive performance.

4. Conclusions

In the three studies just reviewed, two different approaches to the problem of social influences on intellectual style have been attempted. Two studies involved intervention. The point of these two studies was to see whether modification in adult-child interaction would have an effect on a variety of cognitive and social behaviors believed to be related to communication styles. In our study with preschoolers, we found that increasing the complexity of verbal interaction between teacher and child in the context of a nursery school did apparently affect in a positive way certain "distancing" skills (e.g., comprehension, memory, pantomime). The effects were statistically weak—probabilities were only in the .096 to .005 range—but the fact that the *pattern* of effects was consistent with the theoretical predictions tends to increase the credibility of the findings. We must also note, however, that many factors mitigated against strong effects. We did not have complete control over the content of the program, the control children were in good nursery schools that were similar in many ways to the experimental schools, our instructional interactions with the experimental teachers were limited, and the program was in effect for only a short time. Had any of these factors been arranged more favorably, there is at least the chance that our effects would have appeared more robust.

The second intervention study—the infant school—showed more impressively positive results. Here, six months of intensive intervention are apparently producing highly significantly differences including almost nonoverlapping distributions of Bayley scores. There are probably a number of reasons for the relatively greater success of the infant school; we had more complete control over input, the manipulation involved mothers as well as children, there was the enthusiasm that accompanies a new venture, and, of course, the subjects were infants—who, it is reasonable to assume, are more pliable than preschoolers. Unfortunately, the two intervention studies suffer from serious conceptual flaws if we try to take them as proof of our notions of a stylistic dimension of intelligence determined by social experience. The simple fact of a successful intervention—granting that it has been, in fact, successful—does not prove the validity of our ideas. This, of course, is the conceptual weakness inherent in all experimental studies—a point that psychologists often forget. Having data consistent with an hypothesis doesn't prove it.

To make our point we are required to demonstrate the entire chain of mediating events: social experience that is class-related gives rise to a particular style of interindividual communication that determines intraindividual strategies that can affect performance on a range of cognitive tasks. The linear ordering of these events is, admittedly, too simple, and we do expect each step to feed back on previous ones (e.g., success with various kinds of strategies must eventually affect style), but we feel justified in using the simple model as a first approximation.

The third study we described represents an attempt to start clarifying the intermediate steps—at least as our notions relate to preschoolers. So far we are reasonably convinced that there actually are substantial differences in the use of verbal mediation strategies as a function of income level. We can only predict at this point that there will be related social-class effects when we examine communicative competence and performance on nonverbal cognitive tasks. Even then, there will be the possibility that all these tasks are more closely related to psychometric intelligence than to other factors associated with class experience. Given that such effects hold up and still occur in groups of children matched on IQ, we would have more compelling data for our fundamental point of view.

What we would argue is that the reasoning and data we have presented are good enough to justify a closer look and, that, if correct, the idea of the socialization of intelligence has important implications for the practice of early education. We are suggesting a fairly radical departure from current practice. Most programs of early education seem to be based on one of two models. On the one hand are generalizations and extensions of traditional middle-class nursery schools with their emphasis on social-emotional growth, discovery, etc. The implicit model here, we believe, is that the middle-class experience is the best possible environment and deviations from such experience are pathological by definition. The second model is what we would be tempted to call the "Head Start" approach and is premised on the belief that lower-income children have trouble in school because of what they don't know. This strategy generates programs to teach specific items of educational content that are typically acquired by middle-class children by the time they enter kindergarten, but that poor children often have not learned. We see each of these approaches as inherently flawed if applied in an attempt to alleviate lower-income children's school-related disadvantage.

The traditional nursery school may well be the best experience for middle-class children, but only because they do not need help from outside the home to acquire the basic skills they will need in school. For such children learning to get along with other children may be the most appropriate experience they can have. Unfortunately, for children whose early life experience may have been much more communal (Bernstein's "we" over "I" orientation) such experience may be trivial. Such children may actually need to be taught a more egocentric perspective.

Teaching specific educational content on a remedial basis also seems to miss a basic point. What lower-income children do not know compared to middle-class children is interesting only as a symptom of an underlying cause; it is not the source of the problem. If, for example, we could shield a normal child from learning the names of basic colors until he entered the first grade, he would almost certainly know them before the first week was out—with no specific instruction. On the other hand, a lower-income child who had not learned the same colors because of reliance on context-bound communication patterns could be taught the colors and still be disadvantaged.

The program we advocate is based on the assumption that it is possible to analyze the nature of cultural disadvantagement and to intervene on its actual basis. At the heart of cultural disadvantagement, we propose, is the problem of communication. Communication in restricted codes leads to deficiencies in inter- and (possibly) intraindividual communication as well as a disbelief in one's own effectiveness, i.e., the ability to comprehend and modify one's situation. While this combination of predispositions may be both realistic and adaptive in a culture of poverty, it is absolutely destructive in an educational stiuation. We might assume, for example, that in some cases failure in learning to read may result from the fact that a child may not understand that the written word serves as a technique for communication. Formal education involves two basic processes—communication and comprehension—and out analysis suggests that it is in precisely these areas that lower-income children are deficient.

Finally, if our diagnosis is correct, the treatment is specified. It is not essential that any particular set of school-related skills be taught to young children, but whatever is taught must be taught with elaborated verbal communication that elicits complex thought from the child. It might be possible, of course, to teach sets of specific intraindividual strategies related to style, but such an intervention would be unnecessary if, in fact, intraindividual strategies follow from interindividual communication styles. Also, we would not expect such an intervention to be of lasting value because, again, we would be treating symptoms, not the fundamental problem. The only way to have a lasting influence on the child's educational future would be to effect a fundamental change in his view of the world.

Whether such a change can, in fact, be effected remains an empirical question. A decade of remedial education does not seem to have produced any earth-shaking results, possibly because it has been undertaken so far with little real thought to the psychological processes involved. There has been an almost simple-minded faith in the environmental determinants of intelligence—in the broad sense—and in the efficiency of environmental manipulation. We have argued that teaching content on a remedial basis or just placing lower-income children in middle-class nursery school environments does not have long-range effects, nor is raising psychometric IQ a suitable goal. Perhaps, however, a candid appraisal of our successes and failures will teach us to be a little more circumspect in making predictions about simple relations between environmental inputs and behavioral outcomes. The analysis presented herein suggests a complex and indirect route between what we might call a disadvantaged environment and disadvantaged behavior. The connection can only be understood, we propose, when it is viewed in the light of man's social nature.

REFERENCES

Ainsworth, M. D. S. 1973. The development of infant-mother attachment. In B. M. Caldwell & H. N. Ricciuti (eds.), *Review of child development research,* vol. 3. Chicago: University of Chicago Press.

Ainsworth, M. D. S., & Bell, S. M. 1969. Attachment, exploration and separation: Illustrated by the behavior of one-year-olds in a strange situation. *Child Development* 40: 969–1025.

Bandura, A. 1969. Social learning theory of identificatory processes. *Handbook of Socialization Theory and Research,* pp. 213–62.

Beach, F. A. 1961. The descent of instinct. In R. C. Birney & R. C. Teevan (eds.), *Instinct*. Princeton: Van Nostrand.

Bee, H. L., et al. 1969. Social class differences in maternal teaching strategies and speech patterns. *Developmental Psychology* 1(6): 726–34.

Bereiter, C. 1972. An academic preschool for disadvantaged children: Conclusions from evaluation studies. In J. C. Stanley (ed.), *Preschool programs for the disadvantaged: Five experimental approaches to early childhood education*. Baltimore: Johns Hopkins Press.

Bernstein, B. 1960. Language and social class. *British Journal of Sociology* 11: 271–76.

———. 1962. Linguistic codes, hesitation phenomena and intelligence. *Language and Speech* 5: 31–46(a).

———. 1962. Social Class, linguistic codes and grammatical elements. *Language and Speech* 5: 221–40(b).

———. 1970. A sociolinguistic approach to socialization: With some reference to educability. In F. Williams (ed.), *Language and poverty*. Chicago: Markham.

Bissell, J. S. 1973. Planned variation in Head Start and Follow Through. In J. C. Stanley (ed.), *Contemporary education, ages 2–8: Recent studies of educational intervention*. Baltimore: John Hopkins Press.

Bloom, B. 1964. *Stability and change in human characteristics*. New York: Wiley.

Bronfenbrenner, U. 1974. Is early intervention effective? *A report on longitudinal evaluations of preschool programs,* vol. II. DHEW Publication No. (OHD) 74–25.

Bruner, J. S. 1971. *The relevance of education*. New York: Norton.

Bush, E. S., & Cohen, L. B. 1970. The effects of relevant and irrelevant labels on short-term memory in nursery-school children. *Psychonomic Science* 18: 228–29.

Caldwell, B. M., & Richmond, J. B. 1968. The children's center in Syracuse, New York. In C. A. Chandler, R. S. Lourie, & A. D. Peters (eds.), *Early child care*. New York: Atherton Press.

Campbell, D. T., & Frey, P. W. 1970. The implications of learning theory for the fade-out of gains from compensatory education. In J. Hellmuth (ed.), *Disadvantaged child,* vol. 3. New York: Brunner/Mazel.

Carroll, J. B. 1964. *Language and thought*. Englewood Cliffs, N.J.: Prentice-Hall.

Cazden, C. B. 1966. Subcultural differences in child language: An interdisciplinary review. *Merrill-Palmer Quarterly* 12: 185–219.

Dale, P. S. 1969. Color naming, matching, and recognition by preschoolers. *Child Development* 40(4): 1135–44.

Entwisle, D. R. 1968. Developmental sociolinguistics: Inner-city children. *American Journal of Sociology* 74(1): 37–49.

Entwisle, D. R., & Greenberger, E. 1969. Racial differences in the language of grade school children. *Sociology of Education* 42(3): 238–50.

Flanders, J. P. 1968. A review of research on imitative behavior. *Psychological Bulletin* 69: 316–37.

Flavell, J. H. 1970. Developmental studies of mediated memory. In H. Reese and L. Lipsett (eds.), *Advances in child development and behavior*, vol. 5. New York: Academic Press.

Garvey, C., & Hogan, R. 1973. Social speech and social interaction: Egocentrism revisited. *Child Development* 44(3): 562–68.

Ginsburg, H. 1972. *The myth of the deprived child.* Englewood Cliffs: Prentice-Hall.

Greenfield, P. M., & Bruner, J. S. 1969. Culture and cognitive growth. In D. A. Goslin (ed.), *Handbook of socialization theory and research.* Chicago: Rand McNally.

Haith, M. 1972. *Day Care and intervention programs for infants.* Atlanta: Avatar Press.

Harlow, H. F., & Harlow, M. K. 1969. Effects of various mother-infant relationships on rhesus monkey behaviors. In B. M. Foss (ed.), *Determinants of infant behavior*, IV. London: Methuen.

Hernnstein, R. J. 1973. *I.Q. in the meritocracy.* Boston: Little, Brown. 1973.

Hess, R. D. 1970. Social class and ethnic influences on socialization. In P. H. Mussen (ed.), *Carmichael's manual of child psychology*, vol. II. New York: Wiley.

Hess, R. D., & Shipman, V. 1965. Early experience and socialization of cognitive modes in children. *Child Development* 36: 869–86.

Hunt, J. McV. 1961. *Intelligence and experience.* New York: Ronald Press.

Jensen, A. R. 1968. Social class and verbal learning. In M. Deutsch, I. Katz, & A. Jensen (eds.), *Social class, race, and psychological development.* New York: Holt, Rinehart & Winston.

––––––. 1969. How much can be boost IQ and scholastic achievement? *Harvard Educational Review* 39: 1–123.

John, V. P., & Goldstein, L. S. 1964. The social context of language acquisition. *Merrill-Palmer Quarterly* 10: 265–75.

Karnes, M. B. 1973. A quarter of a century of research with young handicapped and low-income children at the Institute for Research on Exceptional Children at the University of Illinois. In J. C. Stanley (ed.), *Compensatory education, ages 2–8: Recent studies of educational intervention.* Baltimore: Johns Hopkins Press.

Keeney, T. J., Cannizzo, S. R., & Flavell, J. H. 1967. Spontaneous and induced verbal rehearsal in a recall task. *Child Development* 38: 953–66.

Keister, M. E. 1970. A demonstration project. Group care of infants. Final Report. Greensboro, N.C.: University of North Carolina at Greensboro.

Kendler, H. H., & Kendler, T. S. 1962. Vertical and horizontal processes in problem solving. *Psychological Review* 69: 1–16.

Kingsley, P. R., & Hagen, J. W. 1969. Induced versus spontaneous rehearsal in short-term memory in nursery school children. *Developmental Psychology* 1: 40–46.

Lawton, D. 1964. Social class language differences in group discussions. *Language and speech* 7: 183–204.

Lehrman, D. S. 1961. Problems raised by instinct theories. In R. C. Birney & R. C. Teevan (eds.), *Instinct*. Princeton: Van Nostrand.

Levine, S., Elzey, F. F., & Lewis, M. 1969. *California Preschool Social Competency Scale*. Palo Alto: Consulting Psychologists Press.

Luria, A. R. 1969. Speech development and the formation of mental processes. In M. Cole & I. Maltzman (eds.), *A handbook of contemporary Soviet psychology*. New York: Basic Books.

Main, M. 1973. Exploration, play, and cognitive functioning as related to child-mother attachment. Doctoral dissertation, Johns Hopkins University.

Money, J., & Ehrhardt, A. 1972. *Man and woman, boy and girl*. Baltimore: Johns Hopkins Press.

Piaget, J. 1971. *Biology and Knowledge*. Chicago: University of Chicago Press.

Rheingold, H. L., & Eckerman, C. O. 1969. The infant's free entry into a new environment. *Journal of Experimental Child Psychology* 8: 271–83.

Robinson, W. P. 1965. Cloze procedure as a technique for the investigation of social class differences in language usage. *Language and Speech* 8: 42–55(a).

————. 1965. The elaborated code in working class language. *Language and Speech* 8: 243–52(b).

Sigel, I. E., Secrist, A., & Forman, G. 1972. Early childhood education project annual report: January 1971–December 1971. Progress Report on Office of Economic Opportunity Grant No. CG-8547-B/2.

————. 1973. Psycho-educational intervention beginning at age two: Reflections and outcomes. In J. C. Stanley (ed.), *Compensatory education, ages 2–8: Recent studies of educational intervention*. Baltimore: Johns Hopkins Press.

Tough, J. An interim report of a longitudinal study. University of Leeds, Institute of Education, Language, and Environment, 1970 (cited in Bruner, 1971).

Vandenberg, S. G. 1971. What do we know today about the inheritance of intelligence and how do we know it? In R. Cancro (ed.), *Intelligence: Genetic and environmental influences.* New York: Grune & Stratton.

Vygotsky, L. S. 1962. *Thought and language.* Cambridge: M.I.T. Press.

Watson, J. 1966. The development and generalization of "contingency awareness" in early infancy: Some hypotheses. *Merrill-Palmer Quarterly* 13: 123–35.

————. 1972. Smiling, cooing, and "the game." *Merrill-Palmer Quarterly* 18: 323–39.

Webb, R. A., Oliveri, M. E., & Harnick, F. S. 1974. The dissemination and evaluation of a style-oriented cognitive curriculum for preschoolers. Submitted manuscript, 1974.

Weikart, D. P. 1972. Relationship of curriculum, teaching, and learning in preschool education. In J. C. Stanley (ed.), *Preschool programs for the disadvantaged.* Baltimore: Johns Hopkins Press.

Weir, M. W., & Stevenson, H. W. 1959. The effect of verbalization in children's learning as a function of chronological age. *Child Development* 30: 143–49.

5

PEER INTERACTIONS IN PRESCHOOL CHILDREN

Esther Blank Greif

A good deal of research on early social development has centered on the relationship between a child and his mother. Clearly, this relationship is an important one; deficiencies in both social and cognitive development seem to result from absence of a consistent caretaker, as in the case of institutionalized children (Rheingold 1956), and from lengthy separations from the caretaker (Bowlby 1974). Research on attachment relationships suggests that development of a mother-child bond is essential not only for early development but for the entire life-span. Despite the importance of the mother-child tie, however, it should not be the only major focus of early child development research. It is reasonable to assume that relationships between a child and other individuals are also essential for proper social development.

If we agree that a child's relationship with his mother is not the only necessary relationship, then we should attempt to identify and determine the effects of the "significant others." Fathers seem to be important, both intuitively and empirically (cf. Hetherington 1972; Lynn 1962). We might also add grandparents, housekeepers, and other adults with whom the child is familiar (e.g., neighbors). These people have generally been neglected in the psychological literature, but there is no reason to suggest that they are insignificant to a child. Moreover, the list of relevant others is not complete. There are two striking omissions: siblings and peers. Siblings seem to have a noticeable effect on development, although the precise relationship is not clear. Finally, we need to examine the effects of peers on social and cognitive development of preschool children. Why should peers be important at all? After all, preschool children are not particularly knowledgeable about other people or about their physical world. Are they too inept to sustain social interaction on their own? Are they completely dependent on adult intervention? The answer to these questions, of course, is no. However, the view that children are not completely dependent on adults, and that they are capable of sustaining interactions among themselves, is a controversial one. In part, the controversy stems from the notion that young children are egocentric and are therefore unable to interact with equals, because of their inability to shift roles. The purpose of this paper is to propose that peer interaction is an essential part of development during the preschool years, and that peer relationships in the early years are not only possible, but are actually necessary. It will be maintained that peer interactions provide opportunities for children to practice their social skills; and further, that peer interaction facilitates and expedites social development in children.

Both theory and research provide support for the view that preschool children are capable of sustained social interactions with peers. Mead (1964) proposed that the notion of the "self," the individual's conceptualization of his own existence, comes only from interaction with others. Mead suggested that the recognition of self-as-object arises under several social conditions, including play and games. An implication from this theory is that early interaction leads to early development of the notion of self. Additionally, Mead viewed thinking itself as a social activity, which can only occur if the individual has first achieved the self-consciousness which results from social experience. Thus, we see that for Mead young children need social experience and social interaction opportunities in order to develop both social and cognitive skills. Similarly, Cooley (1902) suggested that interactions with others are crucial for proper development; and that social experience is interconnected with cognitive growth. According to Cooley, "since the growth of the mind is altogether a social process it is unreasonable to suppose that the outcome can be in any way independent of that process" (p. 16). To achieve social and cognitive advancement, then, children must be in contact with others, including peers.

Role theory (cf. Goffman 1959; Sarbin & Allen 1968), which describes interpersonal interactions in terms of the various roles which people play, also provides a foundation for the view that early social interaction with peers is crucial for development. An individual who does not experience varied social situations may not develop a sufficient repertoire of social roles, and would therefore be less comfortable in the social world. While few roles theorists deal directly with developmental issues, the implication that effective individuals are those who can adapt (i.e., change roles) to different situations leads one to the conclusion that children should be exposed to and should learn a variety of roles, and additionally, that they should be given a chance to practice these roles.

In addition to theory, there is empirical evidence which suggests that peer interaction is important for development. On the subhuman level, Harlow and Harlow (1969) reported that monkeys deprived of peer interactions during their early months showed deficits in social behavior, while monkeys deprived of mothers but allowed to interact with peers showed no deficits. This does not mean that peers are necessarily better than mothers, but it does suggest that early peer interaction may be quite important for development in monkeys, and may even compensate for mother absence. It should be kept in mind, of course, that results from research on development of monkeys are not wholly generalizable to development of humans.

With humans it is not possible to manipulate conditions the way one can with monkeys. However, an interesting human "experiment" reported by Freud and Dann (1951) described a group of six children who had been together for several years, without the benefits of a consistent adult figure. These children were separated from their parents at a very early age (approximately a few months to a year) because of World War II. Thus the children were not only deprived of a parent or consistent care-taker but also were deprived of a stable physical environment. One might expect the traumatic nature of the early experiences to result in deficiencies in many areas of development, particularly the social and emotional spheres. In fact, the children were surprisingly normal. Their cognitive and social skills were both adaptive and age-appropriate. As Freud and Dann state, the "children are, without doubt, 'rejected' infants in this sense of the term. They were deprived of mother love, oral satisfactions, stability in their relationships and surroundings. They were passed from one hand to another during their first year, lived in an age group instead of a family during their second and third years, and were uprooted again three times during their fourth year. . . . But they were neither deficient, delinquent nor psychotic. . . . That they were able to acquire a new language in the midst of their upheavals, bears witness to a basically unharmed contact with their environment" (p. 168). Apparently the children had developed strong bonds among themselves: "It was evident that they cared greatly for each other and not at all for anybody or anything else" (p. 131). These mutual ties seemed to compensate for the absence of an adult attachment figure.

Observational studies conducted largely in the 1930's indicated that preschool children are able and willing to interact with each other (cf. Markey 1935; Maudry & Nekula 1939). For example, Markey (1935) examined imaginative play in preschool children and noticed a large incidence of dramatic play. Parten (1933), in an observational study of nursery school children, also noted that dramatization of home life was a popular activity. These findings all indicate that children are in fact interested in social interactions.

After a few decades in which research on early social development was neglected, there has been a resurgence of interest in the process of social development. Garvey and Hogan (1973) have examined the social speech and behavior of preschool children and concluded that young children are capable of genuine social activity. Mueller (1971) found that preschool children are able to initiate and sustain verbal contacts. Mueller has extended his research on social contact to preverbal children (approximately one year old), and found that while the amount of social interaction is less for this age group, children nevertheless attempt to interact with their peers (Mueller, in press).

Several implications arise from these empirical studies. First, chilren are sociocentric. With both adults and peers, they seem eager to initiate social contact and to sustain these introductions. Further, children seem able to modify their needs to fit with the needs of their peers. Second, the acquisition of interaction skills seems to be a developmental process. Although young children often attempt to get attention from others, they do not always employ appropriate techniques and their attempts therefore fail. Since young children are not as responsive to social cues as older children and adults, the failure rate would be increased when young children interact with each other. Finally, it seems that a coherent scheme or framework for interaction is important for the acquisition of social skills. As with language, children need to learn the social rules. A structure which orders interactions should therefore be a useful tool for young children.

In order to examine children's social interaction skills, and to determine how children achieve social contact, this writer has studied pairs of children in free-play situations. In the study to be reported here, twenty-four nursery school children from middle-class professional families participated. Twelve of the children ranged in age from 3½ to 4½; the other twelve ranged from 4¼ to 5½. There were six girls and six boys in the younger group, and seven girls and five boys in the older group.

A nursery school teacher accompanied three same-aged children from the same nursery school class to the observational area, where the playroom was located (not at the nursery school). All groups contained children of both sexes. When they arrived, the children were greeted by an adult who helped remove their coats and tried to make them feel comfortable. (The nursery school teacher left unobtrusively and went into the observation room.) None of the children appeared disturbed by the new environment, although there were, of course, individual differences in reactions. For example, some children began to explore the new room as soon as their coats were off; others simply stood quietly waiting for instructions.

Next, we prudently took the children to the bathrooms. While this is a rather standard event, there was an interesting interaction pattern during this short "trip." With three children and one adult (whom the children had just met), one might expect the children to talk both to the adult and to each other. Suprisingly, however, there was virtually no conversation among the children. Instead, they all seemed eager to gain attention from the adult. It is interesting to speculate about this; perhaps the adult was seen (correctly) as the source of power and control (cf. Bandura, Ross & Ross 1963). Or, perhaps the children were interested in the new adult as a novel person, and since they were previously acquainted with their peers, they were comfortable enought to attempt contact with the adult. It is also interesting to note that children who didn't need to go to the bathroom came along for the walk, suggesting that they did not want to be left out.

After this diversion the children returned to the coatroom and the adult explained to them that they would be playing some games. Since the children went to the playroom in pairs, a procedure was needed to determine which two children would go first. We decided to make this into a small game by having the children draw straws; whoever drew the short straws (two of them) went to the playroom first. (The other child participated in another study.) The two children with the short straws were taken into the playroom, which contained a variety of toys, and were told they could play with anything they liked. No other instructions were given. They were then left alone for approximately fifteen minutes, with lengths of play sessions varied to avoid interrupting children in the middle of a game. After the first play session, one of the children left the playroom to participate in the other study, and the third child was brought in to complete the second pair. At the completion of the second session, a third dyad was constructed from the previously unpaired children. Thus, each child was in two play sessions with a different playmate each time.

The playroom and an adjacent observation room were connected by a one-way mirror. Video-tape equipment was kept in the observation room, so that children would not be distracted by cameras, and all sessions were video-taped through the one-way mirror. Also, audio tapes were made to facilitate transcriptions of the children's speech. Finally, an observer noted activity which was not recorded by the camera; while video-tapes provide excellent records of events, use of a camera from one direction only results in certain omissions. For example, if a child had his back to the camera, his activity and expressions were not visible. Similarly, if he hid in the corner or behind an object, he would not be recorded on tape. Also, not all verbalizations were picked up by the video and audio tapes. When children crawled behind objects and whispered to each other, their speech could not be heard. The observer tried to reduce the number of these gaps by noting what the child was doing.

The playroom in which the sessions took place was an average size room (approximately 13′ × 10′), which was decorated like a living room, with wall-to-wall carpeting, a sofa along one wall, pictures on the walls, and curtains for the "window" (really a one-way mirror). A variety of toys were scattered around the room. These included two toy telephones, a stuffed snake and fish, a toy stove, a tool belt, a magnifying glass, dress-up clothes, an iron, and a wooden car large enough for two. The wooden car was the largest object in the room (except for the sofa), and was designed specifically for the study. A microphone hung from the ceiling in the center of the room and was partially covered by a stuffed parrot. The room was designed to approximate a normal playroom, with toys similar to those found in nursery schools and homes. Most of the children appeared quite content to be in the playroom, suggesting that the room was designed appropriately.

Before the quantitative analyses were undertaken, speech from the tapes was transcribed to facilitate analyses. To reduce individual differences in comprehension of the children's speech, all transcripts were checked by at least one person other than the original transcriber. Despite this, some speech remained unintelligible—a problem with which the public has become familiar. In some cases, children were whispering or mumbling, as mentioned before. Also, talking while banging an object against another object, which resulted in a loud noise, make it difficult to transcribe the speech. Thus not every sound could be recorded. The symbol "U" was used to denote unintelligible speech.

After all speech (and unintelligible sounds) were recorded, transcripts were divided into utterances, defined as stretches of one person's speech separated by pauses greater than one second, or by another person's speech (cf. Garvey & Hogan 1973). For example, if Child A said,"Wonder what this is . . . (pause greater than one second) . . . hey what is this?", two utterances would be recorded. Similarly, if Child A said, "here's another coffee"; then Child B said "I'm full"; and Child A responded "Here's another coffee," Child A would have two utterances, and Child B would have one.

Video tapes are an extremely rich source of data. Therefore it is necessary (although often difficult) to limit observations to specific types of actions or behaviors. For this study, patterns of children's play were examined. Children's use of role-playing and pretend play was of particular interest, since mutual pretending involves social interaction. Both children need to suspend "reality" at the same time and replace it with the same (or at least similar) constructs.

Since there were no available methods for assessing role-playing from observational data, specific criteria were devised to identify role-playing episodes. Five categories were employed to code each child's activity. These categories were: role-play, role-preparation, pretend play, pretend preparation, and other activity.

Role-play refers to any activity in which the child assumes a distinct identity different from his own. Sometimes this role is clearly stated, as in the example of the boy who declared, "I'm Tarzan." At other times, one can infer a child's role from a combination of his speech and behavior. For example, one four-and-a-half-year-old girl interrupted her house cleaning activities to say to her male playmate, "Don't forget to take your lunch, husband." An interesting exchange occurred between two five-year old girls:

Mary:	Goodbye mom I'm leaving this house going to live with someone.
Lois:	Oh darling you should never go.
Mary:	Goodbye.
Lois:	Never going.
	Come back here darling.
Mary:	I'm going on the train *(note: she pretends that the car is the train).*
Lois:	I want to do that *(note: she seems to forget her role for a moment!).*
Mary:	I'm gonna get on it.
	I got to climb up.
Lois:	You're not going.
Mary:	Yes I am.
Lois:	No you aren't
Mary:	No don't mother . . .

In this brief exchange, two five-year old girls seem to be playing mother and daughter. The conversation is reminiscent of one between a teen-age daughter and her mother.

The second category, role-preparation, concerns a child's structuring a situation for role-playing. Sometimes the children planned what roles they would play: at other times one child announced his role to his playmate. Examples of this category include such statements as: "Let's pretend you're my brother," and "I'll be the mother and you be the father, ok?" Role-preparation does not always precede role-playing, particularly if the roles were already played. Also, attempts to set up roles are not always successful. Nevertheless, explication of the roles ahead of time aided in clarifying the role-playing scene.

Pretend play refers to behavior which was clearly make-believe in that the child was required to pretend something but did not assume a distinct identity different from his own. This does not imply that role-playing is unrelated to pretend. Rather, role-play is a special case of the more general category of pretend play. Examples of pretend include statements such as, "I'm driving to the store," said while sitting on a wooden car. One pair of children prepared a meal, and while eating their nonexistent food, the girl exclaimed, "This ice cream is yummy!" Behavior which seemed like role-play, but which had no clear role referent was classified as pretend play.

Pretend preparation, the fourth category, was analogous to role preparation. Behavior concerned with planning make-believe play was classified as pretend preparation. For example, one child told his playmate: "Pretend this snake is real."

The final category, other activity, was used to classify behaviors not included in the other four categories. These episodes included discussions of the playroom, exchanges about TV shows, especially cartoons, and play which involved no pretending (e.g., peering into the one-way mirror; discovering the camera behind the mirror [only one child noticed it!]). Children also revealed their thoughts to each other. For instance, statements such as "I don't like to be alone," and "I wonder where teacher is" were classified as other activity. An interesting conversation, which lends insight into children's thoughts, occurred between a boy and girl, both age five:

Ann:	Do you play with Barbie dolls?
Ted:	Nah.
Ann:	My friend of mine is a boy and he's six he's nix
	Six nick and and and you know what?
Ted:	What?
Ann:	And he plays with Barbie dolls and dills.
Ted:	Well I don't have any so I don't play with them.
Ann:	Ask your mother to.

Ted:	What?
Ann:	To buy one of the baby dolls.
	Do you have a sister?
Ted:	No.
Ann:	Do you have a brother?
Ted:	No.
Ann:	What do you have?
Ted:	I don't have anything.
Ann:	Dog do you?
Ted:	No.
	Cause dogs ain't allowed in apartments.

At this point the conversation changed; the children became distracted by some toys, and stopped discussing Ted's situation. This short conversation does not involve pretend; rather it is an information exchange, but it is also a social interaction. It is interesting to note the children's conceptions of "having something."

The activity of each child was classified into the five specified categories, using utterances to denote changes from one category to another. Two observers independently coded 33 percent of the sequences into the five categories. Interscorer agreement was computed by comparing the number of agreements to the total number of judgements. Average interscorer agreement was 83 percent.

Examination of the video-tapes revealed a good deal of interaction between children. Even during the first few minutes when children were exploring the new room, they talked to each other about their discoveries.

Quantitive data focused on the involvement of each child in the five categories described above. Since play sessions varied in length

Table 5.1   Mean Percentage of Utterances for Five Categories

	Categories					
Age group	Role play	Role preparation	Pretend play	Pretend preparation	Other activity	Total
3½–4½ (N = 12)	5	4	29	1	61	100
4½–5½ (N = 12)	22	6	18	3	51	100
Total mean (N = 24)	13	5	24	2	56	100

and children differed in amount of speech, the total number of utterances for each child was not constant. To make the data comparable, all classifications were converted to percentages. Table 5.1 presents the mean percentage of utterances in each of the five categories for each age group. Males and females are combined, because there were no significant sex differences in category usage. The table reveals that, across both age groups, an average of 44 percent of the children's utterances were related to imaginative activity, of which 13 percent concerned role play, 24 percent concerned pretend play, and 7 percent concerned role or pretend preparation. It seems that preschool children devote a considerable amount of their time to imaginative activity.

Examination of these results by age groups reveals an interesting trend. The average amount of role-playing was 5 percent for younger children, but increased to 22 percent in older children, a statistically significant difference ($t(22) = 2.83$, p<.01). Concomitantly, the amount of pretend play decreased, from 29 percent in younger children to 18 percent in older children, although this decrease was not statistically significant. As noted above, within age groups there were no sex differences in activity distributions; the percentage of utterances related to each of the categories was the same for boys and girls. Thus, boys and girls participated in the same amount of imaginative play.

The absence of sex differences in frequency of activities does not imply that there were no differences in the content of activities. Since it appeared that boys and girls were adopting different roles, a descriptive analysis of specific activities was made to determine whether some types of play were more common to one sex than to the other.

Table 5.2 contains a descriptive summary of the types and frequencies of roles played. Some children played the same role in both sessions; others used the role in only one session. The table notes only whether or not the activity was performed by a child at least once, in either of the two play sessions. As one can see, there were noticeable differences in the types of roles which children played. The most popular roles were those of mother and father, and in almost all cases girls played the mother and boys played the father. Traditional female roles such as daughter and wife were played almost exclusively by females. Conversely, in addition to

Table 5.2   Common Roles and Frequency of Occurrence

Roles	Female		Male		Total
	Age		Age		
	3½–4½ (N = 6)	4½–5½ (N = 7)	3½–4½ (N = 6)	4½–5½ (N = 5)	
Mother	4	3	0	1	8
Father	1	1	2	2	6
Son	0	0	2	3	5
Daughter	1	3	0	0	4
Fireman	0	2	0	4	6
Baby	1	2	0	0	3
Wife	0	2	0	0	2
Husband	0	0	0	2	2
Bride	0	2	0	0	2

Note: Frequencies represent the number of children who played the role at least once.

father, roles of son and husband were played by males. Thus children not only play roles spontaneously, but they also adopt sex-appropriate roles at a very early age.

As Table 5.2 shows, there was some sex-inappropriate role-playing (e.g., girls playing the role of father), but this occurred only when an appropriate person was absent. For example, when two girls were together, there was no natural male to play father; consequently, one of the girls might play the father role. If both a

Table 5.3.   Pretend Activities and Frequency of Occurrence

Activity	Female		Male		Total
	3½–4½ (N = 6)	4½–5½ (N = 7)	3½–4½ (N = 6)	4½–5½ (N = 5)	
Driving car	4	7	6	5	22
Phone calls	3	5	5	4	17
Treating animals as if they were real	4	3	3	3	13
Fixing car	2	3	2	3	10
Dressing up	1	5	2	0	8
Cooking	2	2	2	1	7
Eating	1	1	3	0	5

Note: Frequencies represent the number of children who engaged in this activity at least once.

boy and a girl were present, however, the boy would play the role of father. It seems that children's choices of roles are determined not only by their personal preferences but also by the requirements of the situation.

A summary of frequent pretend activities is presented in Table 5.3. Sex differences in pretend activities were not as noticeable as they were in role playing. The most popular activity, driving the car, was shared equally by males and females. Similarly, making phone calls was popular among both boys and girls. Playmates sometimes called each other, usually after structuring the situation. Below is an example of a phone conversation between two five-year-old girls.

Jane:	Ding dong ding dong ding dong ding dong Pretend you got it pretend you got it.
Cara:	No pretend I wasn't home.
Jane:	Pretend you were.
Cara:	ok.
Jane:	Ding dong ding dong.
Cara:	Hello.
Jane:	Hello.
Cara:	Hi.
Jane:	Hi how are you?
Cara:	Fine.
Jane:	Well good well I would like to tell you something I called you up for something.
Cara:	What?
Jane:	Um . . . Um I have a new car and see my my friend has an old one bye.
Cara:	Ok I'll drive it over.

As you can see, Jane successfully convinces Cara to join in a pretend conversation, but then Jane finds that she has little to say!

Another activity which children exhibited was taking a stuffed animal and pretending it was real. For example, one pair of children decided to pretend the snake was real; they then proceeded to express fear of it. In several instances a little girl would shriek, "Oooo—a snake!" Her male playmate would comfort her by disclosing that, "it's not real."

Cooking and eating refer to the preparation and serving of something edible, such as coffee, meat, or ice cream. Some of these sequences were extremely realistic; children even paused the appropriate amount of time between bites to chew their "food." Further, after tasting a new food, they often commented on its taste (e.g., "This ice cream was yummy!").

Fixing the car was another popular activity. Although the wooden car was not broken, some of the children used the plastic toys to fix it. This activity was shared equally by boys and girls. Finally, dress-up clothes were used by some of the children, although many ignored them. This activity was more frequent among girls; the two boys who "dressed-up" only tried on several available hats. Girls, on the other hand, explored the clothes more carefully (but few of them actually "dressed-up").

Findings from these observations of free play in preschool children support the views that children are sociocentric, are capable of sustained social interactions, and can benefit from peer interactions. When left alone, all pairs of children employed both verbal and nonverbal (e.g., looking at each other; sharing a toy or activity) techniques of interaction. Even during "solitary" play, when the two children were engaged in different activities, they frequently talked to each other about what they were doing. Also, they often tried to capture each other's attention with phrases such as "Look what I'm doing" and "Wow—look at this!" Thus, children seemed to make active attempts to establish social contact with their playmates.

Children's spontaneous interactions can be classified into several distinct types, as described above. In some instances, children interact simply by having conversations. These talks exemplify an advanced form of interaction in that they do not depend on environmental props (e.g., toys). For example, when one five-year-old girl mentioned her desire to find her teacher and go back to her classroom (a familiar environment), her female playmate asked if she was afraid ("a scaredy cat"). A brief conversation followed, in which the first girl denied being afraid. Other types of conversation depended on children's use of imagination. For example, discussions about the dangers of being eaten by the (stuffed) snake required children to suspend reality and imagine that the snake was real. Children's ability to engage in diverse types of interactions suggests that preschool children have well-developed competencies in the social sphere: they are not simply familiar with different routines and structures for interaction, but are actually able to use the routines and are facile at switching from one to another. Of course there are occasional difficulties; children are not as adept as adults, and sometimes two children are unable to coordinate their routines. For example, in a pretend sequence, Karl said "Goodbye, I'm going to school," assuming his (female) playmate would go along with the pretend. Instead, his playmate replied, "You're already at school," thereby confusing the pretend and disrupting the activity. (In this case the children maintained the contact by beginning a repetitive dialogue in which Karl said "No I'm not' and his playmate responded "Yes you are.") Despite this sort of problem, the sophisticated skills which children exhibit by changing interaction routines are quite impressive.

A fascinating type of spontaneous social interaction occurred in the form of role-play. In these situations, children "played at" (cf. Mead 1964) being someone else. The most popular roles are also the most salient in children's lives; viz., mother, father, son, and daughter. Children seemed to know appropriate characteristics of these roles, and were eager to exhibit them. Results indicated that older children displayed more role-play than younger children, while younger children engaged in more pretend play.

The small amount of role-play in younger children does not suggest that they are socially inept. As we have seen, these children are in fact capable of peer interaction. Instead, we might speculate that role-play is a complex behavior pattern involving the integration of several types of activities, including pretend play, within a rule-following context. While younger children possess pieces of knowledge dealing with daily activities (e.g., cooking, buying something at a store), they seem unable to coordinate all the parts into a specific role. That is, children seem to learn role-related behaviors before acquiring an understanding of the rule systems within which specific behaviors occur (cf. Peters 1958). For example, whereas younger children simply would "cook" food and then "eat" it, among older children the "mother" might cook dinner for the "father." With increasing experience, children exhibit more role-play. Clearly, then, the absence of much role-play in younger children does not imply that they are asocial and egocentric; rather, the small amount of role interaction may reflect a lack of skills in this type of activity.

Three more observations about children's role-playing are noteworthy. First, children do not simply have a specific set of role behaviors which are immutable; instead, children are capable of adapting and modifying their role-play behaviors to fit the situation and the playmate. For example, a girl may play a wife when with a male playmate, but switch to sister when with a female playmate. Second, children not only are aware of the roles they are playing, but they know the complementary roles as well. There are several sequences in which children displayed knowledge of opposite roles. For example, after deciding to play mother and father, a five-year-old "mother" began finding role appropriate items for "father." She gave him a man's hat, then a tie. In this way children support each other in their roles.

Finally, children share their role knowledge and provide feedback to their playmates. Particularly interesting are sequences where one child acts in a manner which the other child considers to be inappropriate (often due to sex roles). An example involving two five-year-olds (boy and girl) is presented below:

Sam:	Look in here. I see you.
	Hey you're dressing up like a man.
	(Note:—Mae is putting on a safari hat.)
Mae:	I know. I want to be a man.
Sam:	You're not supposed to; you're a girl. You're not a man.
Mae:	I know.
	(Sam pushes the hat off Mae's head;
	she tries to put it on him.)
Sam:	Hey!
Mae:	Then you wear this *(gives Sam the hat).*

This feedback operates as a form of socialization pressure; peers teach each other new techniques and share their knowledge of appropriate behavior (not always in a positive, tolerant fashion!). In sum, role-play seems to provide a framework within which children can interact, can exchange information, and can socialize each other.

These observations of the utility of role-play in particular, and peer play in general, lead one go appreciate the social competencies of preschool children. In contrast to the stereotypic view of young children as basically asocial, young children actually seem willing and eager to interact with each other. Pairs of children spend a good deal of time paying attention to their playmates. Further, children are quite adept at different methods of interaction (e.g., simple conversation, pretend play, etc.), and have skills which enable them to initiate and sustain interactions. Thus, the views that children are uninterested in peers and are incapable of peer interaction are not supported. Instead, preschool children seem to possess a good deal of social competence.

Additionally, observations of young children at play suggest that children are able to consider the needs of their playmates. Recently a good deal of attention has been given to young children's inability to understand the perspective of others (egocentrism; cf. Flavell, Botkin, Fry, Wright, & Jarvis 1968). However, research on egocentrism has focused primarily on children's cognitive abilities, without emphasis on the interrelationship between cognitive skills and social skills. In a typical study of egocentrism, children are presented with a situation which they must then describe from the perspective of another individual. Children under age six frequently perform poorly on this type of task. However, naturalistic observations of children at play do not support these findings; rather, they indicate that children can take into account the perspective of their playmates (cf. Garvey & Hogan 1973). Children in the current study demonstrated the ability to modify their own verbal and nonverbal actions in response to their playmates' actions (see samples of conversation in earlier portions of this chapter). Rather than being egocentric, children in fact seem to be aware of and sensitive to the needs of others.

Several implications follow from studies of young children's peer interactions. The current study, in conjunction with previous studies (e.g., Hicks 1965; Reuter & Yunik 1973) and our expanding knowledge of the interactive nature of development, suggest that children can and do benefit greatly from peer experience. When children are with peers they get a chance to try out and practice new behaviors in the presence of others. In addition, they are exposed to new ideas and new skills. Both of these benefits allow children to broaden their experiences with others and to improve their social skills. Peers also help socialize each other; children provide feedback to each other concerning appropriate social behavior. Finally, when interacting with peers, young children have the opportunity to initiate and control their own activities, without adult intervention. This allows them to make use of interaction skills, and to feel a sense of control over other people and new environments.

The potential benefits of peer interactions lead one to speculate about the role of day-care centers and nursery schools in facilitating social development. We have seen that children are quite capable of interacting with each other, and in fact seem eager to do so. Because group situations provide opportunities for children to be together, they can play in important role in early social development. Some opportunities which day-care or nursery school settings can provide are often unavailable in the home. First, children in preschool settings are able to take an active part in the selection of their playmates. Children who remain at home frequently play only with peers who are "convenient"—e.g., relatives and neighbors. These peers may not necessarily be liked by a child. In contrast, children in a preschool can choose their own playmates. Second, there seems to be a qualitative difference between adult-child interaction and child-child interaction. There are certain activities which children can engage in only with peers, just as there are other activities which children can engage in only with adults. Children who have a chance to interact with each other as well as with adults can employ both child-child and child-adult interaction routines. Thus they can use a larger repertoire of activities than can children who interact only with adults or only with peers. Finally, children in a child-oriented setting have the opportunity to experience a sense of control over their world. In a preschool setting, there can be less adult structure and more freedom for children to do as they wish. This includes acting on the physical environment as well as on the social environment. In sum, it seems that preschool centers have the potential to enhance social development, particularly by providing children with the opportunity to interact with each other, and are therefore valuable resources to which we should pay more attention.

SUMMARY

In this paper I have argued that preschool children are socio-centric and are socially competent and can derive many benefits from peer experience. Young children not only possess a respectable repertoire of interaction routines, but further, they can use these skills to sustain interactions with agemates. To maintain that preschool children can only learn from older children or adults is to underestimate the competence of these children. Children can and do learn from each other. They exchange information about the world and themselves; they offer each other suggestions about appropriate ways to behave. The notion that preschool children can learn from one another is an important one, as it provides a basis on which to structure preschool programs. Further, it points to the positive contribution which peers can make to the development of their agemates. By taking advantage of this natural resource, we have nothing to lose and much to gain. As Bronfenbrenner (1967) observes, "In the light of the increasing evidence for the influence of the peer group on the behavior and psychological development of children and adolescents, it is questionable whether any society, whatever its social system, can afford to leave largely to chance the direction of this influence and realization of its high potential for fostering constructive development both for the child and his society" (p. 206). The essential functions of peers in early social development and the role of group-care programs in maximizing peer opportunities for children, can no longer be neglected.

REFERENCES

Bandura, A., Ross, D., & Ross, S. 1963. A comparative test of the status envy, social power, and secondary reinforcement theories of identificatory learning. *Journal of Abnormal and Social Psychology* 67: 527–34.

Bowlby, J. 1974. *Attachment and loss.* vol. II: *Separation.* New York: Basic Books.

Bronfenbrenner, U. 1967. Response to pressure from peers versus adults among Soviet and American school children. *International Journal of Psychology* 2: 199–207.

Cooley, C. H. 1902. *Human nature and the social order.* New York: Scribners.

Flavell, J. H., Botkin, P. T., Fry, C. L., Jr., Wright, J..W., & Jarvis, P. E. 1968. *The development of role-taking and communication skills in children.* New York: Wiley.

Freud, A., & Dann, S. 1951. An experiment in group upbringing. In R. S. Eissler, A. Freud., H. Hartmann, and E. Kris (eds.), *The psychoanalytic study of the child.* Vol. VI. International Universities Press.

Garvey, C., & Hogan, R. 1973. Social speech and social interaction: Egocentrism revisited. *Child Development* 44: 562–68.

Goffman, E. 1959. *The presentation of self in everyday life.* Garden City, New York: Anchor Doubleday.

Harlow, H. F., & Harlow, M. K. 1965. The affectional systems. In A. M. Schrier, H. F. Harlow, and F. Stollnitz (eds.), *Behavior of nonhuman primates.* Vol. II. New York: Academic Press.

Hetherington, E. M. 1972. Effects of father absence on personality development in adolescent daughters. *Developmental Psychology* 7: 313–26.

Hicks, D. J. 1965. Imitation and retention of film-mediated agressive peer and adult models. *Journal of Personality and Social Psychology* 2: 97–100.

Lynn, D. B. 1962. Sex-role and parental identification. *Child Development* 33: 555–64.

Markey, F. V. 1935. Imaginative behavior of preschool children. *Child Development Monographs.* No. 18.

Maudry, M., & Nekula, M. 1939. Social relations between children of the same age during the first two years of life. *Journal of Genetic Psychology* 1954: 193–215.

Mead, G. H. 1934. *Mind, self, and society.* Chicago: University of Chicago Press.

Mueller, E. 1972. The maintenance of verbal exchanges between young children. *Child Development* 43: 930–38.

Mueller, E., & Rich, A. Clustering and socially-directed behaviors in a playgroup of one-year-old boys. *Early Child Development and Care,* in press.

Parten, M. 1933. Social play among preschool children. *Journal of Abnormal and Social Psychology* 28: 136–47.

Peters, R. S. 1958. *The concept of motivation.* London: Routledge & Kegan Paul.

Reuter, J., & Yunik, G. 1973. Social interaction in nursery schools. *Developmental Psychology* 9: 319–25.

Rheingold, H. 1956. The modification of social responsiveness in institutional babies. *Monographs of the Society for Research in Child Development,* 21, No. 2.

Sarbin, T. R., & Allen, V. L. 1968. Role theory. In G. Lindzey & E. Aronson (eds.), *Handbook of social psychology.* Vol. I. Reading, Mass. Addison-Wesley.

6

PROJECT AWARE: A SCHOOL PROGRAM TO FACILITATE THE SOCIAL DEVELOPMENT OF CHILDREN

Phyllis T. Elardo

The purpose of schooling has received considerable attention throughout the history of the United States. In 1974, there seems to be little question about the importance accorded to the role of the school in the traditional areas of reading, writing, and arithmetic.

Dewey (1959), the most influential American educational philosopher, stressed development of the life of the whole child as the goal of education. He said: "The child is an organic whole, intellectually, socially, and morally, as well as physically. We must take the child as a member of society in the broadest sense, and demand for and from the schools whatever is necessary to enable the child intelligently to recognize all his social relations and take his part in sustaining them (1959, pp. 8–9)."

Many people today see a great need to refocus education in the directions that Dewey envisioned many years ago (Kohlberg & Mayer 1972). Recently, the educational establishment has been widely criticized (Silberman 1970; Holt 1964) for overemphasizing cognitive development while allowing the "affective domain" to be slighted. As articulated by Silberman (1970): "education should prepare people not just to earn a living but to live a life—a creative, humane and sensitive life. This means that schools must provide a liberal, humanizing education (p. 114).

Recognizing the concern for affective education, Ebel (1973), the president of the American Educational Research Association, wrote just recently: "Perhaps the reasons so few schools seem to be doing much about affective education is that there is nothing much to be done that is sensible and effective (p. 10)." This failure to formalize teaching strategies and curricular suggestions to develop children's relationships with others should be carefully questioned, for children between the ages of five to seventeen spend from 25 to 40 percent of their time in educational environments.

One of the most important components of the quality of life in the classroom concerns the manner in which teachers help children develop in their relationships with others. However, there is no widely accepted and implemented curricular program in the social or "affective" area, even though all schools list social development as an important goal. In addition, teacher training institutions have failed to provide teacher with courses on how to facilitate the social development of children. This lack of regularly programmed experiences for children in the social area is puzzling. Generally, teachers embrace notions such as "teach the whole child" and "teach children to think," but actual classroom practices do not often seem to reflect these good intentions.

The purpose of the present paper is to briefly review the research literature on the social development of children during the middle childhood years, to discuss the implications of these studies for school intervention efforts, and to describe in detail the author's project, called Project Aware, which represents an attempt to institutionalize and implement a program designed to facilitate social development in children in the kindergarten and elementary school years.

SOCIAL DEVELOPMENT IN THE MIDDLE CHILDHOOD YEARS
The Development of Role-Taking

There has been a concentrated effort on the part of psychologists to describe children's knowledge of the physical world and to discover how they reason and solve problems in the nonsocial environment. Thousands of studies deal with how children learn facts and concepts. There are hundreds of achievement tests set up to measure how well a child reads, adds, and subtracts, and reasons with respect to the physical world. However, there is a paucity of information available regarding the ontogeny of children's understanding of the social world—the world of interpersonal understanding (Wallach 1963). A key aspect of understanding the social environment is the ability to understand the perspective or viewpoint of another person. The gradual differentiation of "self" from "other" is regarded as a major task of early childhood by most psychoanalytic writers (see Anna Freud 1946). Jean Piaget is the developmental theorist who has done the most to explain the process through which children progress in differentiating self from object and self from other. According to Piaget, young children are essentially egocentric; egocentricity in this context refers to an embeddedness in one's own point of view. Piaget (1962) considered the task of surmounting egocentricity of thought to be a central problem in the course of all human development. He also claimed that the concept of egocentricity explains a wide variety of childhood behaviors such as distorted concepts of causality, distorted relational concepts, lack of conservation ability, communication difficulties, and unawareness of differing social perspectives. In terms of young children's relation to the social environment, Piaget believes that they do not have an awareness that viewpoints of perspectives exist other than their own. In Furth's (1969) words, "Thus . . . seeing himself in all things, he is least able to know his self" (p. 113).

Piaget's construct of egocentrism provided the theoretical basis for Flavell's investigations in 1968. Flavell and his associates published a summary of research studies which illustrated the development of children's role-taking and communication skills. The development of role-taking and communication skills were thought by Flavell and his associates to be two important aspects of social behavior which had been to this point relatively unexplored. Their research inquiry began with a review and summary of research studies on role-taking and communication. From this step Flavell constructed a working model of the nature and integration of these two abilities and generated more detailed analyses of the subskills involved in role-taking and communication. Thus the purpose of the early developmental-descriptive work was to provide a tentative description of "what develops when" in the domain of role-taking and communication behavior. The sequence of development of these two forms of social behavior was said to include:

> 1) the general ability and disposition to "take the role" of another person in the cognitive sense, that is, to assess his response capacities and tendencies in a given situation; and
>
> 2) the more specific ability to use this understanding of the other person's role as a tool in communicating effectively with him (Flavell 1968, p. 1).

Several tasks were developed and administered to children for the purpose of assessing these skills at certain ages and to plot a general framework of the ontogeny of both role-taking and communication skills. The data collected by Flavell suggested that older children are generally able to take the role of the other and communicate more effectively with their audience. It was found that children between the ages of eight and ten seemed to be rapidly progressing toward a less egocentric view of the world and were able to use role-taking skills in their social-communicative interactions. Even though Flavell observed a developmental trend over the ages studied, he also notes in his discussion that there was wide variability even at some of the older ages.

The role-taking tasks that Flavell described and reported in 1968 have since been related to aspects of social development other than communication. Selman (1971) investigated the relationship between the ability of the child to take the role of the other and the ability of the child to make qualitatively higher level moral judgments a la Kohlberg (1963). The purpose of Selman's study was to determine whether the ability to take the role of the other is related to higher levels of moral judgment in middle-childhood. Kohlberg has postulated that the ability to take the role of the other is required for higher levels of moral thinking. Specifically, role-taking is a necessary but not sufficient condition for conventional moral reasoning. The sixty children in Selman's study were given two of Flavell's role-taking tasks and Kohlberg's Moral Judgment Scale

(Kohlberg 1963); the children were eight, nine, and ten years of age. The general findings were that the greater ability to take the role of the other was related significantly to higher levels of moral judgment. Selman found that the majority of children who scored at the conventional level of morality also were classified as role-takers. Of the 60 Ss, there were ten subjects who scored low on both the role-taking tasks and the moral judgment scales. Selman did a follow-up study of these ten subjects, and hypothesized that the subjects would acquire role-taking skills before progressing on Kohlberg's Moral Judgment Scale. After one year, five of the ten subjects became role-takers. Of the five subjects who became role-takers, only two subjects scored at the conventional level of moral judgment. These data support the hypothesis that role-taking may be a necessary but not sufficient condition for the development of moral thought.

In the last four years, Selman (1973) has attempted to conceptualize role-taking (which he terms perspective-taking) within a structuralist framework. Selman and others (Selman, Gordon, & Damon 1973) have defined an invariant sequence of four qualitatively different role-taking stages. At each stage "self" and "other" become more differentiated and integrated. Kohlberg (1970) and Selman (1973) concur that Piaget's cognitive stages are a necessary but not sufficient condition for role-taking development; as mentioned they also posit that role-taking development is a necessary but not sufficient condition for moral development. Empirical studies (Selman 1971; Giraldo 1972; Moir 1971) indicate that moral judgment is related to role-taking and to intelligence, but in each study it was found that intelligence and role-taking were more highly related than intelligence and moral maturity. These findings add weight to the argument that role-taking ability is an intervening step between cognitive development and moral maturity.

Flapan (1968) has also studied the ability to take the role of the other during the middle childhood years. In her investigation, she was interested in children's ability to describe and infer the feelings, thoughts, and intentions of people in social episodes. Flapan used sound films portraying episodes of social interaction and presented these to children at various age levels, noting the children's accounts of what had happened and their responses to a specific series of questions. She studied sixty girls aged six to twelve. Several excerpts from a film were shown to the girls and they were asked questions about each episode.

Each excerpt portrayed a variety of feelings, motivations, family relationships, and social situations. The girls were asked to describe each episode in their own words, and their responses were assembled into three categories. The three categories were (1) reporting-describing, (2) explaining, and (3) inferring-interpreting. The observed developmental trends can be summarized as follows: the older girls were more able to give causal explanations and to make interpretations of feelings or to infer thoughts of the characters which were not overtly expressed in the movies. They were also asked to respond to interview questions about the movie. Again there was a developmental trend with younger girls answering more literally and referring to the actual situation, while the older ones were less literal in their interpretations and were able to explain, interpret, and to infer feelings, thoughts, and intentions. Generally, younger girls gave responses that fit into Piaget's perceptual mode: the girls merely reported "what they saw." Flapan's six-year-old subjects offered relatively few interpretations of the feelings or thoughts of the characters in the film. The nine- and twelve-year-olds referred to the feelings and thoughts of the characters in the film more often. This study supports the observation that older children are more capable of viewing situations from the standpoint of the other person. One of the most interesting findings was that wherever there was statistically significant differences between the six-year-olds and twelve-year-olds, there were also statistically significant differences between the six-year-olds and the nine-year-olds. The suggestion from these data is that there is a period of rapid change between the ages of six and nine years of age in children's ability to understand social interactions.

There are many areas yet to be researched sufficiently in the study of the ontogeny of role-taking. Our area is an investigation of the causal factors responsible for role-taking development, i.e., what are the socialization practices necessary for development. Flavell (1963) has suggested that role-taking is facilitated by social interaction:

". . . social interaction is the principal liberating factor, particularly social interaction with peers. In the course of his contacts (and especially, his conflicts and arguments) with other children, the child increasingly finds himself forced to reexamine his own percepts and concepts in the light of those of others, and by so doing, gradually rids himself of cognitive egocentrism" (Flavell 1963, p. 279).

Thus it appears that the decline of egocentrism is the result of verbal interchanges with other people. Recent research supports this hypothesis. For example, Hollos and Cowan (1973) found that there were differences in Norwegian children's role-taking ability as a function of setting. Farm children were low in role-taking scores when compared to village and town children, although all three groups were similar on measures of logical operations. The researchers characterized the farm setting as being relatively more isolated than the village and town environments, with few opportunities for social interaction outside the immediate family. Further research is needed to explore the influence of certain interaction styles on the development of role-taking.

Another major area of inquiry is the relationship of role-taking to other social behaviors such as altruism, acceptance by peers, self-reliance, locus of control, adjustment to the school environment, relationships with parents and teachers, etc. Chandler (1973) has hypothesized that a relationship exists between "persistent social egocentrism and chronic delinquent behavior." He noted that a number of investigations (Anthony 1959; Chandler 1972; Feffer 1970; Gough 1948; Martin 1968; Sarbin 1954; Thompson 1968) point to the proposition that "prosocial behavior is linked to the development of age-appropriate role-taking or perspective-taking skills." Furthermore, people who demonstrate social deviancies are ones who seem to lack an understanding of how their behavior is disrespectful of the rights of others. Chandler (1973) studied the relationship between delinquency and role-taking by comparing the performance of forty-five chronically delinquent boys and forty-five nondelinquent boys between the ages of eleven and thirteen on role-taking ability. The delinquents showed deficits in their ability to take the perspective of others on measures similar to ones developed by Flavell in 1968 as compared to the nondelinquent group. The forty-five delinquents were then assigned to one of three treatment conditions: (a) an experimental group where treatment was focused on facilitating role-taking, (b) a placebo group, and (c) a nontreatment control group. In the experimental group, role-taking was facilitated by a technique which involved drama and video-taping experience. After ten weeks there was a significant increase in role-taking ability by the experimental group only. The other groups did not demonstrate increased role-taking ability. Chandler did a follow-up study after 18 months and found that the treatment group had committed approximately half as many known delinquencies as the placebo and control groups in the same time period.

Although Chandler is quite cautious in his discussion about the interpretation of these findings, the data suggest that role-taking is intimately related to the development of prosocial behavior. Obviously, continued research on the relationship of role-taking to other behaviors is certainly needed.

Role-taking research: Summary and implications for intervention. The development of role-taking during the middle childhood years appears to be an important milestone in the socialization of the child. Flavell (1968) provided a description of "what develops when" in the domain of role-taking skills, and Flapan (1968) has offered descriptive data which add support to the hypothesis that role-taking skills are rapidly developing during middle childhood. Selman and others (Selman 1973; Selman & Byrne 1973; Selman, Gordon, & Damon 1973) have begun to define stages in the development of role-taking and have also begun to document the existence of a relationship between role-taking and moral judgment. Hollos and Cowan (1973) have provided evidence that social interaction is related to the development of role-taking.

It has become increasingly obvious to the author that the school environment has the potential for providing many social interaction opportunities which would promote role-taking ability in children. However, as pointed out above, while the school curriculum contains well-organized and sequenced programs in the cognitive domain, there are reltively few instructional and curriculum suggestions in the affective domain which are well-accepted and implemented.

Bloom (1964) has suggested that the greatest impact on a characteristic can be made during its most rapid period of growth. From the research reviewed in the present paper, it appears that during middle childhood there is rapid growth in the ability of the child to take the role of the other. Following Bloom's reasoning, intervention intended to enhance children's social and interpersonal development during the middle childhood years should be aimed at facilitating role-taking skills. The school environment is quite logically one setting that could be used for this facilitation.

The Development of Social Problem-Solving

Not only is it important to facilitate role-taking during middle childhood, but it is also necessary to develop social problem-solving skills. Such skills include being able to define and understand a problem, being able to consider alternatives to solving a problem, and being able to understand the possible consequences to each alternative.

Bruner (1971) claims that the major source of differences between good and poor learners is in the ways goals are defined and problems are approached. This claim seems to be substantiated by recent research on problem solving which involves an interpersonal conflict (social problem solving). In investigations which have been ongoing for a decade Spivack and Shure (1974) have hypothesized that better adjusted individuals, independent of socioeconomic status and age, are able to verbalize more alternatives to problems and the alternatives are more rational, thoughtful, and less aggressive than the alternatives suggested by less well-adjusted individuals. Spivack and Shure (1974) argue that being able to think of several resolutions to problems is an important step in avoiding interpersonal conflicts.

The relationship between the ability to generate alternatives to problems and behavioral adjustment has provided concurrent validity for the Spivack and Shure hypothesis. Using fifth-graders as subjects, from both low- and middle-class settings, Shure and Spivack (1970*a*) assessed each child's ability to verbalize alternatives to problem situations.

This is a sample problem situation: "Johnny wants his friend to go to the playground with him after school, but his friend doesn't want to go. What can Johnny do to get his friend to go with him?" The youngsters were encouraged to think of as many alternatives as they could to the situation. The same children were rated by their teachers on their behavior in the classroom, using the Devereux Elementary School Behavior Rating Scale, an instrument which measures a child's adjustment to the classroom environment (Spivack & Swift 1967). The finding was that those children who were able to entertain a variety of alternatives were also the ones who were rated as better adjusted by their teachers. The relationship was found in both the low- and middle-class samples.

Further research (Shure & Spivack 1974) has indicated that the problem-solving strategies of normal and disturbed children ten to twelve years of age are significantly different. The children who had been identified as having behavioral problems were found to have a narrower range of solutions, mostly classified as impulsive and aggressive, and were also able to verbalize fewer alternatives. The relationship between behavioral adjustment and problem-solving strategies has also been explored with preschool children (Shure & Spivack 1970*b*). Although the probing procedure for assessing alternatives among four- and five-year-old children was changed to meet the developmental level of the children, a relationship was found between numbers of alternatives and both school adjustment and socioeconomic level. From these studies the correlations indicate that classroom adjustment is related to the child's ability to verbalize alternatives to real-life problem situations. The correlational relationships imply only that increasing a child's number of verbalized alternatives to problems aid his behavioral adjustment or vice versa.

Recently, Spivack and Shure (1974) have reported on three intervention studies. One of the main purposes of these studies was to train children to consider alternatives to problems as well as the consequences of each alternative. Each of the intervention efforts lasted at least ten weeks, with several training sessions each week.

The training sessions consisted of opportunities for children to be questioned about their strategies in real-life problem solving. The most striking finding was that children who showed the most overt behavioral improvement from pre- to posttest were also the children who evidenced the greatest gain in problem-solving ability. The suggestion from these findings is that improving problem-solving ability also improves overt behavioral adjustment. The training was focused on teaching children "how to think" and not "what to think."

Social problem-solving research: Summary and implications for intervention. Although the intervention work reported by Spivack and Shure (1974) has centered on the preschool child, there is a need to explore the effects of intervention efforts aimed at increasing children's ability to verbalize alternatives to problems during their middle childhood years, and to relate this to their overt behavioral adjustment. The data on children in their middle years have indicated that a relationship exists between the ability to verbalize alternatives and behavioral adjustment. However, there have not been any systematic intervention studies to facilitate social problem-solving, using the rationale of Spivack and Shure for children from five to eleven years of age.

FACILITATING THE SOCIAL DEVELOPMENT OF CHILDREN IN SCHOOL: PROJECT AWARE

In conceptualizing and designing an intervention program to foster social development, it was obvious that one target for intervention was the schools, as this setting is one of the most important and potentially accessible environments that influences social development.

The importance of the role of the school has recently been stressed by the Joint Commission on Mental Health of Children (1970). One of the Commission's conclusions was that schools have a tremendous and largely untapped potential for enhancing the mental health of all the children who attend them and for preventing the development of serious emotional problems. According to the

Commission, the promotion of mental health in educational settings should receive as much emphasis as does the treatment of specific emotional and mental disorders.

While there are numerous articles, books, reports, and research studies which point to the need for programs to facilitate development in the affective-social area, there are few models for workable intervention programs. The present effort, labeled Project Aware, represents such a school intervention program. It was designed to foster development in the affective-social area by means of facilitating role-taking and social problem solving.

A Strategy For Formulating a School-Base Program

A major strategy in the design of Project Aware was to create an environment within the school setting in which the social competencies of all children are enhanced. There was little concern with creating a program which would remedy social-emotional problems; that is, the program was thought of as preventive rather than remedial. Indeed, as Kohlberg, LaCrosse and Ricks (1971) pointed out, the best predictors of adult adjustment are the presence of various forms of competence at early ages.

Another consideration in the overall design of Project Aware was that "continuity" should be a major focus. In other words, the program was planned to encompass the kindergarten through elementary school years. In the late 1960's, the evaluations of national intervention programs, such as Project Head Start, had left no question about the importance of continuity of support for children and had renewed everyone's appreciation for the complexity of human development. The personal impact of working in a comprehensive child-development facility for children from six months to eleven years of age (Caldwell 1969; Elardo & Caldwell 1973), designed specifically to provide continuity in the lives of children, convinced the author that any meaningful educational-developmental program for children had to be ongoing for a number of years. It was also obvious from research that the social abilities developing during middle childhood could not be significantly influenced in a few short months—thus another reason for designing a program with continuity.

A third consideration is formulating a strategy for a school-based program was to not only demonstrate that certain experiences would facilitate social development but, equally important, to demonstrate that such a program could be implemented and become an integral part of the school environment. Thus Project Aware was conceptualized as an ecological intervention.

COMPONENTS OF PROJECT AWARE

The Objectives of Project Aware

Project Aware is intended to enrich the school curriculum in such a way as to facilitate children's role-taking and social problem-solving skills. Specifically the objectives of Project Aware are the following:

1. to increase each child's ability to take the role of the other, i.e., to understand the thoughts and feelings of others;

2. to increase each child's ability to be more understanding and acceptant of individual differences, including his or her own individual differences;

3. to improve each child's ability to solve interpersonal problems by being able to define problems, by being able to suggest alternatives, and by being able to understand the consequences of the alternatives to all people involved.

With these objectives in mind, program activities were planned. Project Aware has gone through several phases of development. The first year it was thought of as a separate course within the school day and a time period was allocated four times a week as the Aware group discussion time. The intervention consisted of group discussions led by the principal investigator and teacher. During the second year, the program was blended into the total school curriculum and the separate group discussions became only one part of the Aware Program. The third year has involved further expansion and a more sophisticated research design was employed.

Phase I—The Separate Course Phase

The first step in implementing an educational-developmental program to facilitate role-taking and social problem solving was to plan various social interaction experiences. The most appropriate mechanism for this seemed to be classroom discussions. The initial intervention effort was aimed at planning group discussions which could easily become a certain part of the school day. The idea of having a special discussion time was in harmony with the few commercially packaged programs that were beginning to be marketed (Bessell & Palomares 1969; Dinkmeyer 1970). Although these programs had differing theoretical rationales, their discussion groups were conceptualized as separate courses. Since most teachers had had no experience with this type of educational endeavor, the principal investigator decided that she should work directly in the classroom with the teachers and children to implement the Aware discussions. This also was intended to provide valuable experience for the principal investigator in terms of ideas for discussion topics.

The major purposes of the pilot study (Phase I) were to refine the treatment, to learn how to implement knowledge, to choose and refine dependent measures, to further develop a continuity of support model, and to explore the relationship of the program to other aspects of the curriculum.

During the spring of 1971 the principal investigator became familiar with the small school in which the program would be piloted. Formally labeled "The Center for Early Development and Education," the school was unique because it was an experimental comprehensive child development facility for children from six-months to eleven years of age. The school's population included 65 percent black children and 35 percent white children. Most of the children were from low-income families. There were approximately twenty to twenty-five children in each of the six elementary classrooms.

Observations made in the classrooms during the spring of 1971 revealed that there were few if any occasions during which teachers in the primary grades discussed social problems by exploring alternatives with the children or in which teachers facilitated role-taking development of a systematic basis.

The primary group was chosen as the pilot group for the first attempt to implement Project Aware. The primary group contained children from six to nine years of age in three classrooms. From the research literature cited earlier, this age group was the one where the most rapid growth was likely to occur in role-taking development.

During the first year of implementation, with the assistance of each teacher, the principal investigator began to conduct in-classroom group meetings where an active exchange of ideas on thoughts and feelings, ways to solve problems, and opportunities to take the role of the other were provided. The meetings lasted approximately thirty minutes. In order to assess the impact of the meetings, each of the three primary classrooms was divided into two groups; one was presented with the Aware program and the other was presented with a health and growth program. The principal investigator and the teacher conducted the Aware group meetings and a health and growth teacher taught the other half of each class. The question being asked in the pilot phase was: "What is the effect of the separate Aware course on children's role-taking and social problem-solving abilities?"

The Aware group meetings. A discussion topic was introduced by using some type of stimulus, such as a story, a puppet dramatization, a photograph, a record, a filmstrip, etc. These props provided the stimulus for discussion. The children were given many opportunities to discuss their thoughts and feelings, the thoughts and feelings of others, ways to solve problems, and the consequences of solutions.

The following four examples are representative of several topics covered during the Aware meetings.

1. The leader tells the children the following story. After school some girls were playing hopscotch on the playground. Jean is not able to do as well as the other children and as she loses for the third time she runs away and cries. (The leader asks a number of questions about the thoughts and feelings of the people involved in the story. The children are encouraged to describe alternatives of action for each of the girls involved. The reasons "why" they might act in a particular way are discussed. Each alternative can be role-

played and further discussion of the thoughts and feelings of each person involved is encouraged.)

2. During the art period before the Aware meeting the children are to make "feeling badges." The badges should include a feeling word such as, "mad, glad, happy, excited, surprised, angry," etc. During the Aware meeting, all children should be given an opportunity to choose the badge that described their feelings. The reasons for the feelings should be explained to the rest of the group. At another Aware meeting time each child should be given an opportunity to describe the feelings of another person in the group. Each child should pick out a feeling badge that describes someone else in the group. The reasons for the feelings should be explained.

3. The leader asks the children to suggest ideas for handling themselves in each of the following situations. If it seems appropriate, a few of the suggestions can be role-played. After each situation is presented, the teacher should say:

What would be your thoughts and feelings if you were the person with the problem?

What could you do?

What might happen (what are the consequences)?

Situations:

a. You see some children fighting on the playground.

b. Another person hits you when the two of you are in line to get a drink.

c. You want to make someone feel good about himself.

d. You accidentally break a friend's pencil.

e. You come into class tardy and it isn't your fault.

f. You come into class tardy and it is you fault.

4. The leader tells the following story to the class: Mrs. Smith is the teacher in the fourth-year room. She is ill one day and Mrs. Lee, a substitute, takes over the class for the day. During the math lesson a few children start talking and yelling. This interrupts the lesson and disturbs the group. Mrs. Lee tries to stop the noise but several children say, "You are not our real teacher and we do not have to do what you say." The following questions should be asked:

a. How do you think Mrs. Lee feels? Why? What is Mrs. Lee thinking?

b. How would you feel if you were Mrs. Lee? Why?

c. What should Mrs. Lee do? Why?
d. If you were in the class, what should you do? Why?
e. How do you think the children who are trying to learn the math lesson feel?
f. Why did the children disturb the math group?

After the problem has been discussed, the children are encouraged to role-play alternative endings to the dilemma.

For each Aware session, discussion starters, such as the ones described above, were introduced. The children were encouraged to bring relevant ideas for topics to the group meetings and these were also discussed.

Teachers' meetings. Throughout the year the principal investigator met with the three participating regular classroom teachers to plan Aware discussions and to further explain the rationale for the program. The teachers were given articles to read and relevant materials to consider for use in the meetings. Although the teachers were encouraged to make suggestions for group discussions, there was very little input from the teachers to the program.

Assessment procedures. Subjects were given pre- and posttests. The major dependent variables measured were: role-taking ability, ability to verbalize story alternatives, and the teacher's perception of each child's adjustment in the classroom.

Two role-taking tasks designed by Flavell (1968) were used to assess the ability to "take the role of the other," in other words, to assess each child's ability to shift his or her social perspective. The testing was done individually.

Stories were developed by the principal investigator to determine how many alternatives to everyday problems a child could verbalize and the types of solutions that would be given.

The Devereux Elementary School Behavior Rating Scale (Spivack & Swift 1967) was filled out by the classroom teacher as a pre- and postmeasure. The instrument was chosen as the device for measuring behavioral adjustment in the classroom. There are forty-seven items on the scale and each teacher rates each child on each of the items. For example, the teacher must indicate whether a child engages in teasing and tormenting other children on a five-point scale ranging from "very frequently" to "never."

Results. There was no significant effects after one year. The children, who were from six to ten years of age at the time of the testing, did not make significant gains in role-taking ability nor in the ability to verbalize alternatives to problems nor in the teacher's perceptions of their classroom adjustment. The experimental and control groups scored essentially the same on the three tests.

Discussion. The following interpretations are offered for the lack of demonstrated experimental effect in the pilot year.

The program in the first year was a separate course which was added to the curriculum. Because of the research design, both the teachers and children perceived the program as completely separate and unrelated to the total curriculum. There were also many indications that the teachers did not value the Aware discussions, although they verbalized support to the importance of social development. One teacher tried to withdraw her involvement in the program in the first month of implementation. In the principal investigator's concern for assessing the impact of the program, a situation was created where the teachers did not have to become involved or committed to the Aware program. The principal investigator was always present to help conduct the meetings, and with this situation several teachers found excuses to leave the classroom during the Aware group discussions to make an "important" phone call or run to the office on business. On several occasions two of the teachers indicated that they would sit at a desk close by the circle and correct papers, since they were so far behind in their plans for other areas of the instructional program. During these times the children would continually look to the teacher for approval; the attention of the children was thus divided between what the principal investigator was doing and the cues provided by the teacher.

These observations have implications for auxiliary personnel working in the schools: there is the danger that teachers will perceive the help as separate and unrelated to what they are doing. The most important thing learned in the first year was that no matter what kind of program is introduced into the curriculum there is no question that its success or failure rests in the hands of the classroom teacher. The notion that an outside expert can come into a classroom for a brief period of time and influence development is very questionable.

At the end of the pilot year, several discussions were held with the teachers for the purposes of formative evaluation. The following plans were made: the teachers wanted to continue with the program, but they requested that their entire class be included and that the whole school from kindergarten through the intermediate grades be involved. Even though the teachers had generally not supported the discussion groups, it was considered important to restructure the program, using the teachers' ideas. Both suggestions were consonant with the opinions of the principal investigator—the teacher had to be the major agent of intervention and the people in the total school environment had to provide opportunities to develop role-taking and social problem solving. Thus the program was moving more toward the concepts of Ojemann (1958) who stated: (1) that any approach to influence the social development of children must deal with the total school environment, and (2) that the child's teacher must be the main carrier of the ideas.

Phase 2:   A "Total School Environment" Approach (Fall 1972—Present)

Project Aware was significantly expanded in scope during Phase 2. The thirty-minute discussion groups, which were held twice a week, continued to function as the primary forum—as a "home-base"—for providing certain planned social interaction experiences intended to facilitate the development of children's role-taking and social problem-solving skills. However, the Aware program in Phase 2 was more broadly conceived and implemented. It differed from Phase 1 in several respects:

1) Classroom teachers became more actively involved in the implementation of the Aware Curriculum—gradually they were to assume the principal investigator's role as the major agent of intervention. Furthermore, Phase 2 saw the expansion of Aware-related activities from the thirty-minute classroom meeting into other areas of the curriculum, as well as into the disciplinary practices of the teachers.

The principal investigator arranged to visit each of the eight classrooms twice a week to attend and assist with the Aware groups for discussion.

In-service training sessions for teachers were held once a week.

2) Aware concepts were blended into several other areas of the curriculum during Phase 2. Working with the teachers, several types of enrichment activities were formulated and implemented. For example, in the language arts area, the school librarian compiled several lists of books that had themes that were related to Aware objectives. These books were displayed in the library and used during story time in the library.

On numerous occasions teachers would use materials which suggested Aware themes as stimuli for writing activities. These materials included open-ended stories, photographs depicting conflict situations, open-ended sentences, records, etc.

In social studies, the children in several classrooms prepared "Me" scrapbooks. In the books each child listed his characteristics —height, weight, sex, eye color, skin color, hair color, etc. The children also wrote about how they were the same as other people in the room and how they were different from other people in the room. Another section of the "Me" books contained collages of pictures which showed things that the children liked. The children also added their favorite drawings and favorite pieces of creative writing.

Another social studies unit for the intermediate pupils was on blindness. The children read several books on people who were blind and discussed how blinded people think. The teacher invited three blind children to visit the classroom. During the afternoon visit, the children asked the blind children many questions, watched a wrestling match between blind boys, and exchanged information about how each group learned to read. This experience provided a good opportunity for children to learn more about how it feels to be in "another guy's shoes."

Other social studies units have included topics such as civil rights and the women's liberation movement.

In music many songs with Aware concepts were learned during the course of the year and were included on programs for parents.

In drama, two primary classrooms prepared a skit for their parents which concerned what they were learning in Aware. The skit was about a girl who was teased about not being able to jump rope. After the girl became upset and left the jump-rope area on the playground, several children discussed how she must be feeling and decided that they would try and help her learn to jump rope (this required both role-taking and social problem-solving skills).

3) Teachers were trained to use Aware concepts in everyday discipline situations during Phase 2. When there were behavior problems, the teachers were encouraged to withdraw privileges and, in line with the Aware objectives, the teachers were to ask children how their inappropriate behavior made other people feel. By doing this it was assumed that the child would be placed in a situation where he would be required to engage in role-taking. The teachers were to help the child "verbalize the thoughts and feelings of the other people involved. The children were also asked to think of alternatives for "solving" the problem. Before the teacher terminated the discipline discussion, each child involved was to offer alternatives for solving the problem. The school principal also used the Aware concepts when she dealt with discipline problems.

What was being instituted in these situations was what Hoffman (1971) in his review of moral development, referred to as "other-oriented induction"—being able to discuss the thoughts and feelings of the other. Hoffman (1970) stated that other-oriented induction is the "most facilitative form of discipline for building long-term controls independent of external sanctions" (p. 332).

4) Another way in which Project Aware was expanded during Phase 2 involved the selection of an "Aware Person of the Week." At each group discussion the classroom teacher was given the opportunity to pick a child who had exemplified on the playground or in the classroom that s/he could take the role of the other and could use this understanding in solving a problem. The Aware Person of the Week had his/her picture taken and the picture was put on a special bulletin board.

Description of the Aware curriculum. By the end of Phase 2, four Aware units had been developed. The units are titled: "getting acquainted," "recognizing and understanding feelings," "understanding and accepting individual differences," and "developing social living behaviors: self-reliance and respect and concern for others." During the following summer, one of the teachers who was a strong advocate of Project Aware's objectives offered to help write a handbook of activities. All of the discussion topics, which comprised the above four units, as well as suggestions for expanding the Aware objectives into other areas of the curriculum (the enrichment activities) were thus compiled into a formal handbook (Elardo & Cooper 1977).

The following is a brief description of the four Aware units.

Unit 1: Getting Acquainted. The first few discussion groups each year were used to formulate rules for the meetings and to provide the opportunity for group members to get better acquainted. Rules for the group meetings were suggested by the children and the reasons for the rules were discussed. The teacher discussed the goals of the Aware group discussions with the children.

Unit 2: Recognizing and Understanding Feelings. The activities in this unit were designed to increase the children's awareness of their own feelings and of the feelings of others.

The first few activities of this unit involved encouraging children to label their feelings and to recognize that everyone has feelings. This was done not only in the discussions but was also reinforced in language arts, social studies, music, art, and drama. The other activities in the unit were focused on understanding the reasons for feelings. It was pointed out by the teacher that the causes for feelings are sometimes different. Throughout the unit, children were encouraged to be role-takers by questions from the teacher, such as: How do you suppose John feels? Why does he feel that way? Have you ever had that feeling? Why?

Unit 3: Understanding and Accepting Individual Differences. The purpose of these activities was to help children become better role-takers—to provide them with an understanding of "how it feels to put oneself in the other person's shoes." Throughout the meetings the children switched roles so that they would be able to role-play someone else and to better understand a situation from someone else's perspective.

There were also activities to increase each child's knowledge of his uniqueness and to encourage each child's respect and concern for the individual differences of others. As part of this unit each child prepared a booklet with pictures and stories written about himself.

The enrichment activities included books, writing activities, filmstrips, and records which were centered on exposure to the thoughts and feelings of self and others.

Unit 4: Developing Social Living Behaviors: Self-Reliance and Respect and Concern for Others. The purpose of the fourth unit was to provide opportunities for discussion of social problem situations. The children were encouraged to express their ideas about ways for solving each problem presented in the discussions and to describes the various consequences involved. The technique of role-playing the various alternatives was employed in order to help the children see the problem situation from the perspective of others. Throughout the discussions of the problem situations, the thoughts and feelings of the people involved were a major focus. For example, one problem situation concerned what a child could do if s/he saw a friend take something from the teacher's desk. The options available and the thoughts and feelings of all people involved were discussed.

Another purpose of this unit was to emphasize how the way we act affects other people. The activities were thus aimed at increasing each child's awareness of why one should show respect and concern for others.

The enrichment activities carried the themes of self-reliance and respect and concern for others into other curriculum areas.

Discussion. Two major findings in Phase 2 were that the majority of teachers were willing to become committed to the objectives and could execute activities that would facilitate role-taking and social problem solving. There was no formal (summative) evaluation of the program during this year. The major questions were centered on the success of implementation. Of the eight teachers, only two were somewhat resistant. These two teachers did not consistently become involved in the group meetings.

A third finding was that the objectives of Project Aware could be and were being translated into the total school environment: into other curriculum areas as well as into disciplinary practices. For example, during October, the girls in one of the intermediate classrooms decided that only black girls could be cheerleaders. When several white girls showed up for practice there was a fight and the white girls left. By arrangement the school principal came in during one of the Aware group discussions and dramatically highlighted the conflict by announcing (as in the blue-eye-brown-eye experiment) that, since she was white, only white girls could be cheerleaders. There was then a discussion of the thoughts and feelings of all people involved. One of the black girls broke into tears about her behavior toward the white girls. This experience was planned to place the black girls in "the other person's shoes."

After this session, the teacher and principal investigator planned a number of discussions about the acceptance of individual differences. The focal point for two sessions was a popular record which emphasized brotherhood. The class wrote down the words and discussed the meaning of the song.

Another instance involved a girl in one of the classrooms who had an artificial bladder. The other children continually belittled and ostracized this child, especially when odors developed. During one Aware meeting when this child was out of the room, the situation was discussed with the children. The children took the part of this little girl, while the others in the class teased. The children were then asked to discuss their feelings when they played the role of this girl. The children were very expressive about how another person might feel under these circumstances.

In January 1973, the principal investigator had an evaluation meeting with the teachers. At that time it was a group decision that the principal investigator's involvement could be limited to attending one discussion per week and the teachers would follow through on their own with the second meeting. The decision was based on a suggestion by one of the teachers. This was a significant step since it was an indication of commitment to the program and that the teachers were willing to assume some of the responsibility for the program. In other words, they were becoming the major agents of intervention.

Another indication that the teachers valued Project Aware can be noted for a survey taken in the spring of 1973. Staff members at the Center for Early Development and Education were given an opportunity to list the advantages, disadvantages, achievements, and problems of working in an experimental comprehensive child-development facility. Project Aware was selected by staff members as the most popular experimental project, when compared with a school-wide behavior modification program, an in-service training program for teachers, a language-experience reading program, and an experimental science program.

Phase 3: An Experimental
Study — Research in Progress (Fall 1973-Spring 1974)

During the spring of 1973 personnel from several other Little Rock schools became interested in Project Aware. Two principals were especially interested in the possibility of implementing Project Aware in their schools during the next school year. They said that the development of a school human relations program was one of their greatest needs. Both were principals in intermediate schools (schools attended by nine- and ten-year-old children).

In April, the Aware developmental rationale and curriculum were explained to the administrators in the public school system. The purpose of the presentation was to explore the possibility of offering an in-service training in Project Aware for teachers and principals. At that time the administrators were reluctant to offer an in-service program. However, approval was given to offer a graduate psychology course to principals and teachers who might be interested in the program.

Although the two principals mentioned earlier were interested and ready to implement Project Aware, it was decided that an experimental study should be planned first in order to measure the effects of a "total school" approach on children before beginning a dissemination effort. Thus an experimental study was launched in the fall of 1973. Thirty-three children in several classrooms in School 1 are in the experimental group and 33 children in several classrooms in School 2 are in the control group. The majority of children in the study are nine years of age. The children have been matched on the basis of sex, race, and socioeconomic level of children. Both schools are inner-city schools and 50 percent of their children are bussed several miles daily. Dependent measures will include scores on: role-taking tasks, story alternative tests, sociograms, locus of control measures, rating on teacher perceptions of children's adjustments. The children will also be interviewed in the spring. Post-testing will be at the end of April 1974.

Throughout the planning and implementation of Project Aware in School 1, the school principal has been actively involved. After the goals and components of Project Aware were thoroughly explained to the principal, he discussed the program with his teachers and it was with his recommendation that four teachers signed up for the Aware graduate course in psychology.

The Program at School 1 includes two Aware discussion groups per week, led by the teacher, plus enrichment activities for the children and a meeting with the principal and teachers once a week.

This program has been ongoing for five months as of March 1974, and the teachers and principal are obviously committed to the value of the program. In fact, they suggested making a filmstrip on the program so that each of them could sponsor workshops for other interested teachers.

All four teachers have commented that they feel closer to their students and believe that discipline problems have decreased since the Aware program began. One teacher said: "We really listen to each other, now; I understand more how they are thinking and feeling and they are beginning to understand my thoughts and feelings." Another teacher has said, "The group discussions are terrific. Many of my children never volunteered to talk until we started having Aware discussions. I am so pleased that my slower students seem to feel so comfortable expressing themselves in the discussion groups."

There is little question that the principal and teachers are the major agents of intervention in this school.

DISCUSSION AND CONCLUSIONS

In this paper research on the social development of children has been reviewed and an attempt was made to integrate the findings into a school-based intervention program. The review of the literature made it clear that the development of role-taking during the middle childhood years was an important milestone in the socialization of the child. Also, data on children in the middle childhood period indicated that a relationship exists between the ability to verbalize alternatives to problems and behavioral adjustment, which suggest that by developing social problem-solving skills one could help children deal more effectively with their environment. The school setting was seen as having the potential for providing many opportunities for those social interaction experiences which could promote both role-taking and social problem-solving abilities. The author's strategy in formulating a school-based social intervention program was to design a program for all children in the school between the ages of five to eleven, and to demonstrate that such a program could become an integral part of the school environment.

To date this program, Project Aware, has been implemented to two public schools. Thus it has been demonstrated that a social development program can be designed to include the ages of five to eleven and that the program can be an integral part of the school environment. Research results from Phase 3 of the program will soon be available and will allow a more definitive description of the effects of Project Aware.

Possibly the most important things learned from the author's attempt to translate the child-development research into a natural setting pertain to implementation. Consequently, the following tentative conclusions about factors which facilitate implementation of programs such as Project Aware are offered:

1. Educational interventions which have as goals the development of social competencies should be a part of the total school program, as opposed to separate courses added to the ongoing curriculum. Discussion groups are necessary to provide experiences to promote development but efforts to expand the program into the "total school environment" are also necessary, in contrast to limiting the discussion of concepts to only a certain time of day. In this regard, it is obvious to the author that certain prepackaged materials (filmstrips, tapes, etc.) which are purported to produce gains in social development will not accomplish the task unless there are concomitant changes in teacher behavior throughout the school day.

2. A second factor that was essential for facilitating the implementation of the program was the author's familiarity with the school setting. As Sarason (1971) explained, the person proposing a change must become very familiar with the "culture" of the school. There is no substitute for learning about schools than actually living

in them. In order to facilitate implementation it was necessary to help the teachers implement the objectives, not only in the group discussions but also in other areas of the curriculum. It was found that it is very easy to tell people what to do but more difficult to *help* them do what has been suggested. The interaction of the principal investigator and teacher in the natural setting produced mutual understanding that was invaluable, and, in the process, the credibility of the principal investigator was enhanced. Unless one has been a classroom teacher or has worked rather extensively in a classroom, many educators feel that people outside the system do not understand their problems and therefore cannot be much help. This feeling is probably justified, as unless one has had to cope with some of the everyday problems that teachers are faced with, there are unrealistic expectations about what can be implemented in a school.

3. A third factor which facilitated the implementation of Project Aware is that the principals in the two settings were involved and committed to the concepts. There is little question that the efforts to change certain aspects of the classroom environment would have been only minimally successful without the full support of the principal.

Likewise, the role of the teachers cannot be minimized. In both schools, several teachers have been very vocal in their support for Project Aware. Without the help of these teachers the program could not have been implemented.

Additionally, the author's experiences while working in the schools have brought into sharp focus several critical issues. The major questions that teachers and principals have asked when the developmental rationale and curriculum ideas of Project Aware have been presented and are being implemented are: How do you discipline a child who is not a role-taker? How do you discipline a child in light of the child's development? What do you say and how do you react to a child who when asked to verbalize alternative solutions to a problem can only recite violent ones? What is a growth-producing situation for such a child? These questions are ones which carry implications for research from practice.

In conclusion, it is only disconcerting but shocking to realize what is happening in American schools today: students are displaying more and more physical and verbal abuse toward teachers, many teachers rely solely on corporal punishment to control classroom behavior, and reports of stealing and extortions are commonplace. These are all indicators of a tremendous need for human relations programs in the schools. We cannot afford to say there is nothing sensible and effective that can be done—we must develop some alternatives!

REFERENCES

Anthony, E. J. 1959. An experimental approach to the psychopathology of childhood autism. *British Journal of Medical Psychology* 32: 18–37.

Bessell, H., & Palomares, U. H. 1969. *Human development program.* Los Angeles: Vulcan Binder.

Bloom, B. 1964. *Stability and change in human characteristics.* New York: Wiley.

Bruner, J. S. 1971. *The relevance of education.* New York: W. W. Norton.

Caldwell, B. M. 1969. A Special Facility for Child Development and Education. A proposal submitted to the Research Division, Children's Bureau, Social and Rehabilitation Service, U.S. Department of Health, Education, and Welfare, April 1969.

Chandler, M. J. 1972. Egocentrism in normal and pathological child development. In F. Monks, W. Hartup, & J. DeWitt (eds.), *Determinants of behavioral development.* New York: Academic Press.

————. 1973. Egocentrism and antisocial behavior: The assessment and training of social perspective-taking skills. *Developmental Psychology:* 326–32.

Dewey, J. 1959. Moral principles in education. New York: Houghton-Mifflin (first ed., 1909).

Dinkmeyer, D. 1971. Developing understanding of self and others. Circle Pines, Minnesota: American Guidance Service.

Ebel, R. 1973. The future of measurements of abilities II. *Educational Researcher* 2: 5–12.

Elardo, P. T., & Caldwell, B. M. 1974. The Kramer adventure: A school for the future? *Childhood Education* 50: 143–52.

Elardo P. T., and Cooper, M. 1977. *AWARE: Activities for Social Development.* Menlo Park, Cal.: Addison-Wesley.

Feffer, M. H. 1970. A developmental analysis of interpersonal behavior. *Psychological Review* 77: 197–214.

Flapan, D. 1968. Children's understanding of social interaction. New York: Teachers College Press, Columbia University.

Flavell, J. H. 1963. *The developmental psychology of Jean Piaget.* New York: Van Nostrand.

—————. 1968. *The development of role-taking and communication skills in children.* New York: Wiley.

Freud, A. 1946. *The ego and the mechanisms of defense.* New York: International Universities Press.

Furth, H. G. 1969. *Piaget and knowledge: Theoretical foundations.* Englewood Cliffs, N.J.: Prentice-Hall.

Giraldo, M. 1972. Egocentrism and moral development. Doctoral dissertation, Catholic University, Washington, D.C.

Gough, H. G. 1948. A sociological theory of psychopathy. *American Journal of Sociology* 53: 359–66.

Hoffman, M. L. 1970. Moral development. In P. Mussen (ed.), *Carmichael's manual of child psychology.* New York: Wiley.

Hollos, M., & Cowan, P. A. 1973. Social isolation and cognitive development: Logical operations and role-taking abilities in three Norwegian social settings. *Child Development* 44: 630–41.

Holt, J. *How children fail.* 1964. New York: Pitman.

Joint Commission Mental Health of Children. 1970. *Crisis in child mental health: Challenge for the 1970's.* New York: Harper and Row.

Kohlberg, L. 1963. The development of children's orientation toward a moral order, I: Sequence in the development of moral thought. *Vita Humana* 6: 11–33.

—————. 1970. From is to ought: How to commit the naturalistic fallacy and get away with it in the study of moral development. In T. Mischel (ed.), *Cognitive development and epistemology.* New York: Academic Press.

Kohlberg, L., & Mayer, R. 1972. Development as the aim of education. *Harvard Educational Review* 42: 449–96.

Kohlberg, L., LaCrosse, J., & Ricks, D. 1971. The predictability of adult mental health from childhood behavior. In B. Wolman (ed.), *Handbook of child psychopathology.* New York: McGraw-Hill.

Martin, M. 1968. A role-taking theory of psychopathy. (Doctoral dissertation, University of Oregon) Ann Arbor, Michigan: University Microfilms, No. 68–11, 957.

Moir, D. 1971. Egocentrism and the emergence of conventional morality in preadolescent girls. (Master's thesis, University of Canterbury) Christchurch, New Zealand.

Ojemann, R. H. 1958. The human relations program at the State University of Iowa. *Personnel and Guidance Journal* 37, 199–206.

Piaget, J. 1962. Comments on Vygotsky's critical remarks concerning *The language and thought of the child,* and *Judgment and reasoning in the child.* Attachment to L. S. Vygotsky, *Thought and language.* Cambridge, Mass.: M.I.T. Press.

Piaget, J. 1969. *The language and thought of the child.* New York: Meridian Book, World Publishing (first ed., 1955).

Sarason, S. 1971. *The culture of the school and the problem of change.* Boston: Allyn and Bacon.

Sarbin, T. R. 1954. Role theory. In G. Lindzey (ed.), *Handbook of social psychology.* Cambridge, Mass.: Addison-Wesley.

Selman, R. 1971. The relation of role-taking to the development of moral judgment in children. *Child Development* 42: 79–92.

––––––. 1973. A structural analysis of the ability to take another's social perspective: Stages in the development of role-taking ability. Paper presented to the Society for Research in Child Development, Philadelphia, March 1973.

Selman, R., & Byrne, D. 1973. Manual for scoring role-taking in moral and non-moral dilemmas. Unpublished manuscript. Harvard University.

Selman, R., Gordon, A., & Damon, W. 1973. The relation between stages of social role-taking and stages of justice conception in children ages four to ten. Paper presented to the Eastern Psychological Association, Washington, D.C., May 1973.

Shure, M., & Spivack, G. 1970*a.* Cognitive problem-solving skills, adjustment and social class. Research and evaluation report. Philadelphia: Department of Mental Health Sciences, Hahnemann Medical College and Hospital.

––––––. 1970*b.* Problem-solving capacity, social class and adjustment among nursery school children. Paper presented at the Eastern Psychological Association, Atlantic City.

––––––. 1972. Means-ends thinking, adjustment and social class among elementary school-aged children. *Journal of Consulting and Clinical Psychology* 38: 348–53.

Silberman, C. E. 1970. *Crisis in the classroom.* New York: Random House.

Spivack, G., & Shure, M. B. 1974. *Social adjustment of young children.* San Francisco: Jossey-Bass.

Spivack, G., & Swift, M. 1967. *The Devereux Elementary School Behavior Rating Scale Manual.* The Devereux Foundation, Devon, Pennsylvania.

Thompson, L. A. 1968. Role playing ability and social adjustment in children. (Doctoral dissertation, University of Southern California) Ann Arbor, Michigan: University Microfilms, No. 69–4547.

Wallach, M. A. 1963. Research on children's thinking. In H. Stevenson (ed.), *Child psychology. Sixty-second yearbook of the national society for the study of education.* Chicago, Illinois: University of Chicago Press, 236–72.

Index of Names

(Pages in boldface denote articles in this volume.)

Library of Congress Cataloging in Publication Data

Hyman Blumberg Symposium on Research in Early Childhood
   Education, 4th, Johns Hopkins University, 1974.
   Social development in childhood.

   Papers from the 4th Hyman Blumberg Symposium on
Research in Early Childhood Education, held Mar. 7–9,
1974.

   Includes index.
   1. Education, Preschool—Congresses. 2. Interaction
analysis in education—Congresses. I. Webb, Roger A.
II. Title.
LB1140.2.H94 1974   372.21   77–4778
ISBN 0–8018–1946–6
ISBN 0–8018–1947–4 pbk.